D1035382

MISTER,
You Got Yourself a Horse

MISTER,

You Got Yourself a Horse

Tales of Old-Time Horse Trading

Edited, with an introduction, by
Roger L. Welsch

University of Nebraska Press   Lincoln and London

Copyright © 1981 by the University of Nebraska Press
All rights reserved
Manufactured in the United States of America

◄ The paper in this book meets the guidelines for permanence and durability
of the Committee on Production Guidelines for Book Longevity of the
Council on Library Resources.

Library of Congress Cataloging in Publication Data

Welsch, Roger L.
  Mister, you got yourself a horse.

  Bibliography: p. 207
  1. Horse trading (in religion, folklore, etc.)—United States.   2. Horses—
Legends and stories.   3. Tales, American.   I. Title.
          GR105.5.W44   398.2'4529725   81–436
ISBN 0–8032–4711–7   AACR1

First printing: 1981
Second printing: 1982
Third printing: 1984

For Jenny

"You can shear a sheep many times, but you can only skin him once."

John Klein, sheepshearer

Contents

Preface   ix
Introduction   1

Part I: The Traders

The Reverend Finmore's Slightly Excitable Mare   25
Making Camp by a Cornfield   34
Slade's Hot Dapple Gray   37
Dang Fool Deals   41
Horseface Kartek's Bull Windy   45
I Pulled Out to See a Little More of Arkansas   55
New-fangled Farming   60
Elmore Walker's Ramble on the Plains   65
Old Man Ganter's Hospitality   72

Part II: Horses

Lou and Dexter Find the Gate   87
I Just Give Her a Good Whalin' with a Stay Chain   89
Cocaine for the Dummy   92
Look That Team Over Pretty Carefully   102
Croughan's Puller   105
Trading according to Hoyle   107
Bargains   110
The Good-as-Gold Gelding   119

Part III: Some Trades

Tricks of the Trade   125
Ailing Horses and a Sick Owner   131
The Most Amazing Case of Buttons   134
The Old Arsenic Treatment   139
All the Ribs on One Side   147

Corking a Pelter 155
The Bay with One Flaw 156
The Stump Sucker 158
A Genuine Freak 161
Trading by Moonlight 163
The Roan That Didn't Look So Good 166
Croughan Goes to Court 168
Coming into Glanders in a Bad Way 177
The Heaves Story 178
He Isn't a Kicker, Is He? 180
In Her Cups 182

Part IV: Racers

Old Parity 187
The Famous Shooting Star 194

Glossary 203
Bibliography 207

Preface

When the work of the world was done with genuine horsepower and men traveled in the saddle, a sound knowledge of horseflesh was serious business; it was a ready source of entertainment too. The farming country of Nebraska was opened by the railroads, and the railroads carried its crops to market, but, a hundred years ago, all the work on the farm and all local hauling were still done with horses. Farmers and townsmen who did not breed their own stock had to buy horses or trade for them. Just as the local merchant looked to the drummer to keep him supplied with calico, the farmer whose plowhorse had come up lame would pause to talk when a roader, (an itinerant horse trader) with his string of nags and plugs and mules, stopped his wagon at the gate. Working with horses every day, most men fancied themselves experts, and few could resist the challenge of a trade. Trading horses was a kind of recreation, like betting on races; and, as Mark Twain said of horse races, it was difference of opinion that made horse trades.

By the time the last of the road traders were old men, in the 1930s, all the work was done with machines, horses were toys, and the roaders were long since out of a job. Rudolph Umland, director of the Federal Writers Project for Nebraska, remembered the skillful stories told by an uncle who had been a roader operating out of Beaver City, Nebraska, and sent his fieldworkers out to interview horse traders. The stories in this volume are a result of that effort to add horse-trading narratives to the inventory of material collected by the Federal Writers Project (FWP) in Nebraska. But these stories were nearly lost.

The Federal Writers Project was a part of the Works Progress Administration (WPA), which was in turn a part of Franklin Delano Roosevelt's immense network of relief programs meant to turn the tide of the Great Depression. The Federal Writers Project was designed to employ writers, teachers, scholars, and researchers; throughout the Depression decade the fieldworkers of the Federal Writers Project gathered and squirreled away a huge body of material that has delighted folklorists and historians ever since.

By 1942, when the Federal Writers Project was closed, its ten thousand workers nationally had produced 120 publications in less than eight full years of effort. The most famous were the volumes of the American Guide Series, one for each state and each of the principal cities of the United States.

Even more important perhaps are the thousands upon thousands of files the state offices left behind, unpublished. They lie in library basements, in historical society archives, even lost in government storage buildings. Some were stolen or destroyed. The raw data that remain, however, represent the most thorough survey of American culture ever attempted. Now, more than forty years after they were collected, the materials still capture the attention of scholars.

In part this is because of the timing of the project. In 1935 it was still possible to interview Civil War veterans and former slaves, homesteaders and Oregon Trailers, Indians who remembered the Little Big Horn, and horse traders who had plied their trade in the days before the automobile.

The Nebraska project was especially fruitful. It produced more books per capita than any other project in the country, and the literary quality was unusually high. Lowry C. Wimberly, founder and editor of the prestigious literary journal *Prairie Schooner* at the University of Nebraska, had wide-ranging influence on the Nebraska project. He recommended the best of his students for open jobs and saw to it that many of those associated with the *Schooner* also worked on the Federal Writers Project. Weldon Kees and Rudolph Umland were two who later developed literary reputations apart from the *Prairie Schooner* and the Federal Writers Project in Nebraska; the best-known alumnus of the Nebraska project was Loren Eiseley, a *Schooner* poet who later achieved international distinction as an anthropologist and essayist.

I have been using Nebraska's rich FWP files for a number of books and studies (notably, *A Treasury of Nebraska Pioneer*

Folklore) and have found remnants of the collection in the most unlikely places and in the most deplorable conditions. I have found tall-tale files being converted into mouse nests in the basement of buildings at the University of Nebraska at Omaha, for example, and files momentarily stalled in Washington, D.C., in 1940 and still there in a file drawer today. The most frustrating searches have been for the vast bodies of material that are hinted at in one place but that have not been found. I had found, for example, frequent reference to a huge collection of Nebraska tall tales—along with tantalizing samples—but I simply could not find the actual collection.

One day a friend mentioned that he had heard Jim Potter of the Nebraska State Historical Society read a couple of hilarious pioneer tall tales from a manuscript he had run across in the State Archives. I recognized the samples as tales I had previously seen described as being from the collection. I called Potter immediately and then drove to the Nebraska State Historical Society at full speed. He had found the file I had been hunting for years.

It was while working with those files that I came upon the horse-trading file, a collection I had never seen mentioned before. The stories were fascinating to me—and might, I surmised, be of interest to other readers too.

I offer my thanks to the Federal Writers Project workers who assembled these fine materials; I can imagine the futility and frustration they must have felt in seeing their work lost for four decades. As always, I thank the Nebraska State Historical Society and especially Jim Potter, who helped me find the texts. Lynne Ireland read my manuscripts, offered helpful suggestions, and was tolerant of my sensitivity to those suggestions. Rudolph Umland kindly shared with me his memories of the Federal Writers Project in Nebraska, giving insights to the collection and preparation techniques of the fieldworkers that would otherwise have been totally inaccessible to me. Debra Japp did heroic work as my research assistant, finding dozens of obscure bits of information I was almost certain she could never find.

INTRODUCTION

Farmers on the Great Plains lived a life of isolation one hundred years ago. Today we can see hundreds of strangers a day simply by turning on our television sets or by watching the automobile traffic out of our front windows. Back then, only three or four strange faces might appear in a year, and the sight of a stranger entering the farmyard (once it was determined that he was not an immediate danger) was a rare and exciting occurrence. When the stranger was an itinerant horse trader, offering not only a social exchange but also the opportunity for a battle of wits, the possibility of financial gain, and the certainty of some horse talk, his appearance took on the importance of a first-rate social event.

The classic encounter between the farmer in his dooryard, at first presenting a suspicious or even hostile face to the world, and the voluble and worldly-wise horse trader is central to most of the stories in this volume. For both farmer and trader, the motivation of a good many of the trades is not only money or a better horse but the excitement of the trade itself. Victory or defeat, of course, is a result of a contest, and money or a better horse is a handy way of keeping score.

In the nineteenth century, trading goods of all kinds was a part of American life far beyond anything we can imagine today. European visitors commented in their journals on two distinctive and ubiquitous American habits: spitting and trading. Virtually every American male spit, with remarkable disregard for propriety. Like spitting, trading was a universal convention in the America of the eighteenth and nineteenth centuries. Captain Frederick Marryat commented, in his *Diary in America,* upon "the ruling passion of the country—the spirit of barter, which communicated to the females, as well as to the boys. . . . I heard of an American, who had two sons, and he declared that they were so clever at barter, that he locked them both up together in a room, without a cent in their pockets, and that before they had *swopped* for an hour, they had each gained two dollars a piece." [P. 146]

1

Today, most trade is not trade at all but purchase. We go to a store and exchange money, a symbol for things, for actual things—tomatoes, a bicycle, a house, a song. America today so heavily depends on this system that it is hard for many people to imagine another. Thus the American traveler is frequently confused or even offended by bargaining—the system used, for example, in the markets of Mexico. The American feels that the seller should set a single definite price and stick with it, but in a sense the market in Mexico operates more honestly than the American supermarket. A woman uses her time (and of what value is that?) to gather reeds (of what value?); she uses more of her time—still of indeterminate value—to make a basket; then I show up at her stall in the market to buy the basket (which would be of what value to me?). The basket has no single, definite value. When we bargain in the market, it is not to cheat each other but to determine between us what the value of that basket is.

But at least one of the commodities in that kind of arrangement is relatively constant in its value—the money. The situation gets a lot more complicated when the system is that of barter, exchanging one item for another, or trade, exchanging one item (plus "boot," something extra thrown in) for another of the same item. Now we have *two* items whose value must be determined in the negotiations of the traders.

If a farmer was trading a wagonload of corn for a new plow or a tailor a suit of clothes for a wheel of cheese, there was clear room for bargaining to establish the relative values of the items. How much corn is a plow worth? How much cheese is a suit worth? Those are honest questions of adjustment and compromise, and it is entirely possible in a trade like that for both parties to come out ahead. At the conclusion of the exchange the tailor is glad to be rid of one of his large supply of size forty-nine, amply checked yellow suits and to acquire a magnificent quantity of his favorite cheese; he feels he has won a real bargain, and indeed he has. At the shake of the hands the dairyman is relieved to be parted with so much of his overstock of cheeses, and he is certain that he will win the heart of the Widow Franklin in his new yellow suit with the

2

reversible vest. In short, in a trade like this, both parties feel rightly that they have come out ahead. Both have won.

But when two men trade horses, they are exchanging the same commodity. Each believes he has won after the trade, but by all the precepts and presumptions of logic it is certain that at least one has lost. But the pervasive spirit of deception in horse trades, especially in those that were remembered and retold as stories, virtually guaranteed that both parties had lost. Probably within days each trader was to be disagreeably surprised.

There were of course those situations in which one trader was looking for a plow horse in exchange for his carriage animal, or perhaps a bay to match one he already owned. *Then* there was the potential for a trade that left both parties content. It is also a fact of the art of narration that it is the interesting trades, the ones with major losses or victories, deceits and manipulations, that make the best story. They are therefore the ones that have persisted in the memories of the traders and found their way into Federal Writers Project notebooks.

Earl Conrad wrote a book, *Horse Trader,* about his father, who was an incorrigible trader of the old, "tough luck" school of trading. He got burned his share of times, as every trader did, and yet he traded and traded and traded. He lost money, was cheated, had fair horses swapped from under him for snides, had wagons kicked to shreds and suffered a few wounds himself, was forced to feed and house useless animals for years at a time before he could unload them on some other unsuspecting dupe. So why did he do it? Because, he said, "Rookin' a man for a few bucks more'n a hoss is worth'll do the liver more good than Scott's emulsion" (p. 24).

Yet he was never cheated in our understanding of the word—never short-changed without the victim's knowledge and against the victim's will. Conrad's father knew what was going on. He concurred in it, he agreed with it, he participated in it, he practiced it, he pursued it, *he reveled in it:* "Father's constant use of words like 'skinnin',' 'skunkin',' 'trimmin',' helped me to grasp what these horse transactions were all about. It was a game, a tussle" (p. 19).

If trading became a habit and a sport, it was partly because money was a rare item, and in value it was simply not to be trusted as much as a horse, a jug of moonshine, or a bolt of cloth.

Alan Lomax in *The Folk Songs of North America* records a spoken text from the song "The State of Arkansas":

> But I didn't like the work, nor the food, nor the swamp-angel, nor his wife, nor none of his children. So I went up to him and told him, "Mister, I'm quitting this job. I want to be paid off." He says to me, "All right son," And he handed me a mink skin. He says, "That's what we use for currency down here in Arkansas." So I took it into a saloon to see if I could get me a pint of whisky. Put my mink skin on the bar, and be durned if the bartender didn't slip me that pint. Then he picked up my mink skin, blowed the hair back on it, and handed me three 'possum hides and fourteen rabbit skins for change.

It pays, when you are trading commodities in the absence of money at a fixed value, to make your horse (or mink hide) look as good as possible. From glanders to botts to bull windy, the spectrum of equine diseases, injuries, faults, and bad habits is astonishing (see the Glossary). And, for virtually everything from blindness to old age, with the possible exception of a missing leg, there was a cosmetic cure that would conceal the defect long enough to fool the unwary. Youth spots could be added with Easter egg dye (applied with eggs or biscuits), tooth cups could be recut with acid, and even a missing tail could be replaced with a false one. Some cures were startlingly simple, while others were amazingly complex. And no alteration was considered out of bounds. Horse trading was Yankee ingenuity at its lurid worst.

Knowing that any trader would try to disguise the faults of his horses led a man to be cagey. Thus arose the strategy of the horse trade—to my mind, one of the most fascinating elements of the stories in this book—which became as tradi-

4

tional as an ancient ritual, as formal, subtle, and complicated as a chess game.

Note in "The Reverend Finmore's Slightly Excitable Mare" or "Cocaine for the Dummy," for example, the subtlety of the opening play. Anyone who made it known that he wanted to trade would be at an impossible disadvantage; it would be assumed that he had some *reason* to trade—probably a bad horse. Therefore, the trading session had to be opened in such a way that neither party seemed to start it and neither seemed to want to continue it, even if one of them made his living as a horse trader. The coy maiden being courted couldn't hold a candle to the skills of such horse traders.

A trader might ask for cows or hogs (like William Cole in "Bargains") or play the role of a potential settler; and when he declared an end to the proceedings because he simply "didn't want to trade that badly" was when the trade was most intensely desired.

Another apparent contradiction in tales of horse trading was the universal and pervasive spirit of honesty that dominated these crooked deals. Even though each party to a trade knew that he was cheating the other and was in turn probably being cheated, dishonesty was absolutely forbidden, sort of. If the buyer asked about an infirmity that the horse did indeed have, the seller could not deny the fault outright. He could evade the question or give a deceptive answer, but he would not lie baldfaced. In fact, it was considered a point of honor to declare the animal's faults, but in such a way that the buyer would not understand the true significance of the Delphic words until it was too late to cancel the deal. So the owner of a balky horse would issue the caveat, "You'll be surprised to see the way he works," the surprise being that he would not work at all.

Nor was there much in the way of promoting one's own wares or disparaging those of the other gent: one trader said that, when the other man started to knock his animals, the trader knew he was hot for a trade. Leading statements were cast out, subtle remarks were made, but every conclusion was left tacit. Once the actual trading began, the subtleties fled,

5

and there was open talk of virtues and faults and money to boot, and hard positions were assumed by the traders.

And the conclusion, in brilliant contrast to the opening moves, was abrupt, distinct, and expressed. An observer would have been hard pressed to find exactly where the casual conversation ended and the actual bargaining began, but he would have had no trouble whatever spotting the precise moment the deal was closed. There was perhaps a handshake or a meaningful word—"Deal!" "Done!" "Sold!" "You got you a horse!"—and the two bargainers quickly retreated, each eager to evaluate his purchase and to escape the moment the other man discovered the imperfections of his own new mount.

The human mind has a remarkable capacity for compartmentalizing: the profligate sinner is capable of being totally blind to his own error while noting and condemning the very same transgressions in someone else's behavior. In these horse-trading stories, for example, how often do we see the roader outraged that he has been the victim of a bull windy with a nose stuffed full of sponge or an exhausted nag brought to life with a dose of cocaine! When the moralizing trader finally gets around to remarking that he has just unloaded a totally worthless piece of horse flesh himself, it will often be with a sense of justice: this rascal who would have cheated him has wound up cheated himself.

How fortunate it is for honesty, you may say, and how sad for human interest that the horse traders are now gone. But in a way they are still with us under another guise—that of the used-car dealer. There are still the shallow pretensions of honesty and the underlying baserock of deception. A 1963 Plymouth is sprayed with new-car smell from a can, and while both the seller and the buyer know that the smell is like the white wedding gown of "Good-time Annie," it is a part of the whole sham that is understood to go along with used cars. When the commodities in trade are the same, whether horses or cars, the implicit intention of the exchange is an unequal trade.

Some of the strategy and fair play of the horse trade is, to be sure, absent from the modern automobile trade, because the buyer comes to the seller, and the clear opening move—"I'm looking for a 1970 Dodge"—immediately puts the buyer at the seller's mercy, and the Blue Book system of pricing cars has removed some of the bargaining from the hands and mouths of the litigants. But there are still enough dedicated tire-kickers on the buying end and wheeler-dealers on the selling end of used-cars to keep everyone honest and the pace lively.

But it is in the wares themselves that the horse trader and the used-car deal are most alike. Both the horse and the automobile constitute the second largest family purchase and possession, subordinate only to the home or farm. Most significantly in this regard, both the horse and the car are depreciating properties; most other things of any size and value that a family invests in, especially the home or farm, can be anticipated to increase in value. But used cars and old horses (unless they are classics or put out to stud) can only be less valuable when you sell them than when you buy them. Further, almost all the money that goes into the upkeep of the machine and the animal—feed and gas, veterinarians and mechanics—can be considered good money after bad.

The horse, moreover, served as a mobile symbol of wealth, just as the automobile does in America today. Of course there were other symbols too—a good carriage instead of a lowly farm wagon, a frame house instead of a soddy, a windmill rather than a simple well—but the horse could be ridden to town, in sight of the most cynical detractor. There was plenty of latitude for judging your neighbor. There were as many types and conditions of horses as there are of automobiles.

Perhaps this explains two other parallel phenomena: because the horse and car are indeed very large purchases, carrying immense weight of prestige and price, they are of singular importance to the male of the family, who usually handles the trade; and because they are both notably poor bargains (even while they are necessities), they are traditionally targets of contempt, disgust, frustration, and fury from the wife of the family, television advertisements notwithstanding.

I also like to think that cars and horses are of the same personality: unreliable, malicious, expensive to maintain,

7

prone to overheating in the summer and slow starting in the winter, and notoriously uncomfortable as a mode of transportation. And yet both the car and the horse have a way of inveigling themselves into the lives—if not the hearts—of their possessors (who, too often, become the possessed).

An analogous characteristic that is rarely considered in comparing the horse and the car is the factor of the two in pollution. Today we all know that the automobile is a major contributor to air pollution as well as visual pollution, but we forget that the horse once offered precisely the same problems to the cities, where manure sometimes piled up in gigantic mountains, and the stench brought tears to as many eyes as smog ever has.

A horse is as complicated as a car, and just as a bad set of ball joints in a car (apparently made of the most precious metal known to man) can be good cause to unload the dog with the concomitant risk of assuming in the next vehicle an even worse fault, like a cracked block, a case of the glanders or a tendency to kick could be good reason to trade off a horse in the vain hope of acquiring an animal with a lesser handicap.

Such a horse is recorded in James M. Bailey's *Life in Danbury,* written in 1873, just a short time before the events occurred that are recorded in this collection.

> I don't really believe a yellow horse is any worse by nature than a bayhorse, or a white horse, or a horse of any color or combination of colors; but our judgement of things in this world is often liable to be influenced by our prejudices. For this reason, perhaps, I cannot look upon a yellow horse with any feelings of delight.
>
> A yellow horse was standing at the depot in Washington the time I came down the Shepaug road. Looking at the animal as he felt around casually with his hind foot for his owner's brains, my mind reached back to the home of my childhood.
>
> It seemed so blessed to lean back in the seat, and with partly closed eyes give myself up to reveries retrospective.
>
> I remember quite distinctly the day my parent brought home a yellow horse; in fact, I can without much difficulty pick out any day of the eight which that animal passed in our society. He was

8

a comely beast, with long limbs, a straight body, and eyes that would rival those of an eagle in looking hungry.

When he came into the yard we all went out to look at him. It was an evening—clear, bright, and beautiful. My parent stood near the well holding the animal by a halter. We had a dog, a black and white, and if there ever was a dog who thought he had a head stowed full of knowledge it was that dog.

How plainly I can see him approach that yellow horse, to smell of his heels. He ought to have got more of a smell than he did, considering that he lost the greater part of one ear in the attempt. It was done so quick that it is possible we would not have known anything about it, had the dog not spoken of it himself.

He never smelt of that yellow horse again. The flavor wasn't what he had been used to, I think.

Three days later when he was turning around, to speak to a flea near his tail, as is customary with dogs, that yellow horse unexpectedly reached down and took a mouthful of spinal joints out of the dog's back, and the mortification from being thus caught preyed so heavily upon the dog's mind that he died in a minute or two.

That evening mother interested father with an account of Caper's death while he was waiting for her to replace the collar the yellow horse that afternoon had snatched from his best coat.

And thus time passed. But the horse lost none of it. There wasn't a neighbor within a half mile of our house but bore some mark of that animal's friendship. Like death, he was no respecter of persons. He never stopped to inquire whether a man was worth a million dollars or ten cents when reaching for him. He may have had some curiosity about it afterwards but he never showed it.

Finally people came to avoid him when they met him on the street. I don't think they did it purposely, but it seemed to come natural to them to rush through the first doorway or over the most convenient fence when they saw him approach. This inexplicable dread communicated itself to the very dogs on the street, but before they had come fairly to understand him, he had succeeded in reducing the price of a winter-breakfast luxury to almost a mere song.

After that they looked up to him with the respect exacted by a Hindoo god with two changes of underclothes, and no dog within three blocks of us would think of going to sleep at night without first coming over to see if that horse was locked up. It was instinct, probably.

My parent never enjoyed a single day of the eight he was the sole possessor of the animal. He nipped away some portion of him every once in a while. My parent was not a profane man, but he was sorely tempted to be every hour in the day. The man who lived next to us was a professional swearer. He owned a horse that was a model of goodness in every respect—as gentle as a lamb, and as lovable as a girl of sixteen. My father could never understand this. He always spoke of it as one of the inscrutable ways of providence.

There was only one person that had anything to do with the animal who came out of that fiery ordeal unscathed. He was the hired man, and he owed his salvation to a misfortune. He was cross-eyed. He was a great source of misery to that yellow horse. The misinformation of his eyes was calculated to deceive even smarter beings. The beast kicked at him a few times when he was evidently looking the other way, but that was just the time he was bearing one eye strongly on him, and he missed; and when he really was not looking was just the time the beast thought he was, and so it went through the entire eight days, both stomach and heels yearning for a morsel of him but never getting it.

I am sure there never was another such horse to kick and bite. He did it so unexpectedly too. He would be looking a stranger square in the face, apparently about to communicate some information of value, and then suddenly lift his hind foot, and fetch the unsophisticated man a rap on the head that would make him see seventy-five dollars' worth of fireworks in a minute.

He would bite at anything whether he reached it or not, but in kicking, he rarely missed. He could use any leg with facility, but prided himself mainly on the extraordinary play with the left hind leg. With that limb he would break up a political meeting in five minutes and kick over the entire plan of the campaign before the last man got to the door.

The very air about our place was impregnated with camphor and the various new kinds of liniments. The neighbors came around after dark, and howled for the blood of that yellow horse

10

like so many Indians clambering for a pint of New England potash.

Matters commenced to assume a critical form. The people wanted the animal killed, and cut open so they could get back their things.

And so my parent determined to shoot the beast, but at the last moment his heart failed him. Pity triumphed, and he sold him to a man from a distance, and it was such a great distance that none of us were able to attend his funeral two weeks later, although earnestly invited to do so. He left a wife and three interesting children, and was struck just above the right temple, I believe. [Pp. 90–95]

In a society that depended so much on horses as did pioneer Nebraska, business in horses was brisk. Thus the tales in this collection do not typify only isolated or unusual events clustered around a few rare professional traders or told to us by the rare and unusual narrator.

Anyone could be a horse trader, of course—the casual amateur might be as fanatical as the professional—but in this collection we see primarily the activities of the professional roader. Barn traders were usually livery stable owners who not only housed and rented animals but also sold and traded them. While the barn trader was always regarded as a shrewd businessman, there was also the formidable reality that he had to live in his community and would have to face again and again, year after year, the people with whom he did his trading.

The roader, on the other hand, was the Gypsy of his trade. The roader occasionally passed through the same region at intervals of one or two years, but there was always the possibility that the roader you were trading with would never be seen in the area again. That cast a certain aura of finality over all transactions.

Indeed, the life and style of the roader was apparently so well established that the same patterns recurred again and again. The patterns will be recognized in the following tales, but they were also faithfully outlined in a folksong entitled "The Horse Trader's Song" with an economy of language typi-

11

cal of folk poetry. The song was published in Vance Randolph's *Ozark Folk Songs,* volume 3, as it was originally learned by Fred Woodruff of Arkansas in 1900 and sung by him to the collector in 1941. It thus reflects precisely the period when the traders of this collection were working.

"The Horse Trader's Song"

1. It's do you know those horse traders,
   It's do you know their plan?
   It's do you know those horse traders,
   It's do you know their plan?
   Their plan it is for to snide you
   And git whatever they can, (2×)
   Lord, Lord, I been all around this world.

2. They'll send their women from house to house
   To git whatever they can,
   O yander she comes a-runnin', boys,
   With a hog-jaw in each hand,
   Lord, Lord, I been all around this world.

3. It's look in front of our horses, boys
   O yander comes a man, (2×)
   If I don't git to snide him
   I won't get nary a dram,
   Lord, Lord, I been all around this world.

4. O now we stop for supper, boys,
   We've found a creek at last, (2×)
   O now we stop for supper, boys,
   To turn out on the grass,
   Lord, Lord, I been all around this world.

5. Go saddle up your snides, boys,
   And tie 'em to the rack, (2×)
   The first man that gets 'em
   Will pay us to take 'em back,
   Lord, Lord, I been all around this world.

6. Come on now, boys,
   Let's go git a drink of gin (2×)
   For yander comes the women, boys,
   To bring us to camp agin,
   Lord, Lord, I been all around this world.

The road trader, once common enough to have been the butt of the easy jokes in that song, now survives only on paper in the records of the Nebraska Federal Writers Project and in a few similar archives. The principal problem with the Federal Writers Project materials is that we are working with them forty or forty-five years after the fact of their collection and eighty years after the fact of the trades themselves. The traders who told these stories were pioneers—they were born in the 1850s and 1860s, and they were doing most of their trading before the turn of the century, when farmers were just beginning to abandon horses for steam and internal-combustion-engine tractors. We have little background information about the storytellers or the fieldworkers, and some of the surviving records are fragmentary.

The few fact sheets we have are tantalizing. Fortunately, the best and most productive horse trading storyteller of the Nebraska Federal Writers Project, Lew Croughan, was interviewed meticulously by Harold J. Moss, one of the best of the Federal Writers Project fieldworkers. Moss interviewed Croughan on 1 May and on 25 and 28 October 1940. His biographical notes about Croughan have survived; the portrait they give is at once powerful and pathetic.

By the 1930s Croughan had fallen on hard times; Moss found him living in "bachelor's quarters—3 dingy drab rooms over a carwrecking establishment" at 2227 O Street, Lincoln. At the interview "a small dog, a cross between a Spitz and wire-haired terrier, after extending a noisy and trifle hostile reception, resumed its position underneath its master's great, leather upholstered chair. Cigarette papers and tobacco were arranged conveniently on a small center table directly in front of Mr. Croughan's chair and within easy reach."

Croughan was "a great bulk of a man, towering over six feet," Moss reported in his notes. "Upstanding figure, erect and well poised but not the over-bearing type. Broad full rounded chubby features and large head. Rather rosy, smooth-shaven complexion, gray moustach, partially bald. A man of the world, travel, educated and a shrewd judge of people and human nature. Easy to meet, neighborly and a ready talker but with

13

some reserve and caution. He impresses one as having been a large scale operator in his time."

Croughan was born in Iowa in 1865, Moss learned, and came to Nebraska as an infant. He began his life as a trader in 1879, when he was thirteen years old. In 1881, about sixteen and large for his age, he set out with a team and wagon for Montana.

In 1885 he returned from Montana to Nebraska, where he fell in with a sharpshooting horse trader by the name of Abe Sissler. Up to that time he had developed no particular technique in horse trading, but he learned fast from the foxy Sissler, who was a believer in the school of experience, no matter how costly—to the other fellow.

After a winter when Sissler and his wife managed to skin young Croughan out of everything but his eye teeth, they set out together on a horse-trading tour. That trip laid the groundwork for Croughan's future horse trading ventures, and Sissler actually reversed his tactics of the winter and allowed Croughan to accumulate seven old skates and a linchpin wagon. The fact that those old bone racks could hardly hold up their own harness made little difference, for the helpful Mr. Sissler, now entirely disposed to see his student apprentice do well, emptied his entire bag of horse-trading tricks into the successful dealing of those broken down plugs. That served to round out young Croughan's preliminary education.

What an apt pupil he proved to be is demonstrated in the story entitled "Cocaine for the Dummy," wherein he a short time later returned and outsmarted the unsuspecting Sissler to the tune of a hundred dollars.

He was learning a few new tricks which were unknown even to Sissler. Now, well launched on a horse-trading career, Croughan took to the road in warm weather and shuttled back and forth between Nebraska and surrounding states in the late eighties and through the nineties, dealing in hundreds of horses and mules.

In the early 1900s he became interested in real estate, abandoned the horse-trading business, and proceeded to amass a small fortune—almost fifty thousand dollars. In the hectic

14

postwar days he lost it all as quickly as he had made it and in the same manner—real estate. All but bankrupt in the 1920s and faced with the problem of making a living and recouping his fortunes, Moss reports, "he managed to assemble a covered wagon outfit and some horse trading stock and once again he set out, much as he did in 1879, in the role of a nomadic horse trader. For six years or more he roved over the state until he reached the age of 70. By this time horse trading was on the way out and he was forced to retire."

The few remaining horses that made up the bulk of his belongings were sold under the hammer for the few dollars they would bring, and he faced the future practically penniless. Not content, however, to give up and admit defeat he busied himself selling various items, mostly by pitch work—low pitch, principally—that is, haranguing sidewalk and street corner crowds from ground level. "Horse trading," he told Moss, "was a fine art, but is rapidly becoming a lost one."

He was poor, old, alone, and forgotten in an age of automobiles and youth. Croughan died in Lincoln on 8 June 1946, six days after his eighty-first birthday. The cause of death reported in county records was "senility"; and, curiously, his birthplace was listed not as Iowa, but as Memphis, Tennessee. His name, moreover, was not Lew Croughan as listed by Moss, but Luke Croughan. It is impossible this long after the fact to know whether the name change was a simple misunderstanding on the part of Moss or the records officers or the use of a nickname.

The horse trader tended to be a solitary figure, trusted by no one, trusting no one. He did not enjoy much respect while he was practicing his trade—and, it must be admitted, usually with good reason. It is hard to imagine that, still alone, now aged and tired, the wily roader would talk as freely and articulately with a fieldworker from the Federal Writers Project—a possible government snoop—as these tales suggest. But the fieldworker's visits meant that the trader could again remember and recount those stories that constituted the substance of his life—to interested, respectful ears, and with the real hope that the stories would be preserved in print.

15

We cannot know how many other horse traders there were like Croughan, with stores of tales just as rich. It is fortuitous that the brief facts of Croughan's life, and his hoard of stories, have survived. What little we know of Croughan was uncovered by Harold J. Moss, a practiced storyteller himself. Rudolph Umland, director of Nebraska's Federal Writers Project, told me on 11 September 1979, that Moss had come to the project as a drummer, a drygoods salesman. Drummers, like horse traders, made a living by their skill with language and were notorious for spinning a good yarn. I had wondered how much Croughan's stories might have been changed in Moss's retelling. But Umland, in a letter to me dated 18 August 1979, indicated that, because the fieldworkers were carefully trained and Moss was conscientious, his transcriptions were probably quite accurate. Umland remembered Moss very well:

> Harold Moss died in the early 1950s—his body was found frozen under the snow on an island in the Platte River near Ashland. He was one of the best story gatherers we had on the project. Some people can recall better the things they see, some the things they hear. I remember how impressed I was by Harold Moss's ability to recall what he heard. Shorthand or a recorder wasn't necessary in his case. He could recall conversations and talk verbatim for weeks.
>
> I can still see his thin face all aglow with enthusiasm when he first told me about an old horse trader he had met. It must have been in late 1940 in the basement of old University Hall. I was hopeful that he could gather enough material for a pamphlet on the old horse traders we used to have in Nebraska.
>
> ... Moss was a speedy writer. He wrote his stories on yellow legal-size pads in longhand during a talk session and then had a typist in the office type a first draft. He made corrections on this as the typist made frequent errors trying to read his handwriting. Then a second draft was typed and I imagine it's this second draft that's in the file. No further editing, or polishing, or revisions on the horse trading stories were done to my knowledge. . . .
>
> I believe Moss was quite accurate in taking down the words of the person he was interviewing. . . . I doubt that the stories reflect anything of Moss himself. I think the talk of people generally in the 1930s was more literary in style than the talk of

16

people today but I don't remember Moss's talk as being that way especially. Moss had good ears and was a good listener.

We asked the workers to take down the talk as it was given and I believe Moss did that to the best of his ability. . . . I can't recall that any of the interview material, except what we used in the two or three pamphlets called "Pioneer Life In Nebraska," ever reached an editing stage. If it had we probably would have limited our editing to merely cutting out "repeats" or repetitions.

Of course the fieldworkers could not reproduce an informant's words exactly. They wrote transcriptions on the spot, lacking the tape and video recorders that characterize today's fieldwork in folklore. They left out the coughs and sneezes and lapses of memory that surely were there. They probably added words here and there and left out a few of the more offensive phrases one might expect from horse traders. The effect of the intermediary translator—the fieldworker—cannot be neglected. The real danger is to overestimate the stylistic contributions of the Federal Writers Project fieldworkers and staff. My own first impression of these texts was that they had been substantially altered and improved, as folklore collectors had frequently done in earlier days. But the guide manuals and instruction sheets issued to the Nebraska workers are as rigorous, clear, and professional as anything in circulation in graduate folklore programs today. For those of us who have been convinced that the scientific study of folklore is a postwar development, sections like the following from the Federal Writers Project field manual are startlingly in tune with modern thought:

> Folklore is a body of traditional belief, custom, and expression, handed down largely by mouth and circulating chiefly outside of commercial and academic means of communication and instruction. Every group bound together by common interests and purposes . . . possesses a body of traditions which may be called its folklore. Into these traditions enter many elements, individual, popular, and even "literary," but all are absorbed and assimilated through repetition and variation into a pattern which has value and continuity for the group as a whole.

Although in most cases it is impossible to establish the origin of a piece of folklore, we want to know as much as possible about its source, history, and use, in relation to the past and present experience of the people who keep it alive. This information enables us to understand the function and meaning which folklore has for those who use it and so enhances its interest and significance for others. Just as a folk song or folk tale cannot be said to have a real existence apart from its singing or telling, so in all folklore collections the foreground, or lore, must constantly be related to the background, or life.

In helping supply this living background, the data compiled for the social-ethnic studies will be of great value. At the same time the personal histories and interviews compiled by folklore collectors can be of equal service in social-ethnic studies. [Works Progress Administration files, Nebraska State Historical Society]

Fieldworkers were directed to copy all accounts verbatim, to submit thorough background notes on the informants and their materials, and not to improve the texts at all. In short, the directions are models of folklore field collection. If the collection and typing of the texts in Nebraska were supervised carefully, the stories were very well preserved, and we have before us remarkably detailed and accurate versions of the stories the horse traders told—of stories told by skilled raconteurs.

For their lack of education, the horse traders show remarkable narrative skills. They develop gripping suspense and surprise in their stories; they draw their characters with a fine brush and with considerable humor; they laugh at themselves, draw modest lessons and morals from the related events, and use careful and striking diction.

In the first tale of the collection, "The Reverend Finmore's Slightly Excitable Mare," in which Lew Croughan trades and then back-trades with the Reverend Phineas Finmore, we have an example of the verbal and narrative skills that pervade all of the material of this collection and most other of the horse traders' art. Croughan describes his adversary with selected, significant details: his undertaker's stride, his voice of organ tones, his black frock, the gesture of tapping the tips of his

18

fingers together. I suspect that the name Phineas Finmore is Croughan's invention, and it too fairly rings of sanctimony.

Croughan laces his tale with humor—" 'She is a noble creature' (he meant the horse, not his wife...),"—and both Croughan and the preacher use oratorical maneuvering to win the day: Croughan feigns a slip of the tongue—"If you could show me this 'plug'—I mean mare"—and Finmore throws Croughan completely off balance by being principally concerned not about the worth of the animal but rather about its sex!

Croughan scarcely expected to surprise his audience with his conclusion, for back-trading constitutes by far the most common motif of all horse-trading stories. Instead, in the style that characterizes story telling of a century ago, the mirth and suspense is in the way the story is told. There is a slight hint of what is going to happen in Croughan's opening lines, in which he tells us that he never has had any luck with teachers—and of course preachers. The humor and power·of the tale is in the rich description and character development of the preacher and his wife, and the horses.

How does it happen that we find such talent in a horse trader? The answer is not only simple but direct and essential to the understanding of the tales themselves: good storytellers make good horse traders; good horse traders make good storytellers. The talent of the horse trader was not simply knowing animals but, even more, knowing people—how to develop and hold their interest, how to manipulate words and situations subtly, how to relieve tension with humor, how to live by one's wits.

It is difficult for us to understand the dimensions of the lowly horse trader's eloquence. That difficulty is in part a result of the decline of eloquence in general since the nineteenth century. Today oratorical fireworks like William Jennings Bryan's "Cross of Gold" speech are considered more laughable than moving. But the most skilled of creative writers look to the folk mouth for a turn of phrase. The occasional rural practitioner of Old Speech whom the fieldworker encounters will leave him gasping for breath and most assuredly wishing for the relative calm of academic debate.

Popular studies of horse traders center inevitably and understandably on the verbal skills of the traders. William R. Ferris, Jr.'s "Ray Lum: Muletrader" *(North Carolina Folklore* 21 [1973]:105–19) contains thirteen pages of Lum's words, two pages of Ferris's scholarly treatment. Ferris's film of the same title shows us Lum not so much as a trader and auctioneer but as a raconteur in his tack shop and at the auction ring. Ferris quotes Ray Lum, "I just found out how they make an auctioneer. They vaccinate them with a victrola needle when they are five years old." And the observer is not struck by the action of the trade but by the verbal trickery of the trade and its recounting. Lum, for example, tells of trading a mule to a man who returned the next morning to complain that the mule had died overnight. "Died?" blustered Lum incredulously. "He never once did that when *I* owned him!"

B. F. Sylvester in "Hoss Tradin'," an article that appeared in the *Saturday Evening Post* (6 January 1934, p.12) described the life of the nineteenth-century Missouri Valley horse trader, and he like other authors turned again and again to the striking language of the traders themselves: "I wouldn't own a house where I couldn't smell the barn," for example. And the reply of a trader to the charge that one of the horses he had traded the previous day must be blind because he kept walking into things like the barn and the fence. "Well, he ain't blind," the trader explained. "He just don't care."

The pages of Earl Conrad's *Horse Trader* are like lists of epigrams:

> You don't have to tell a cat what to do with a mouse. [P. 48]
>
> Son, if you're a hoss dealer you might just as well get the best of the deal. [P. 48]
>
> A great hoss in her day. Ain't the best workhoss, but she's wonderful human bein'. [P. 62]
>
> We were very close friends of his so he shot at us first. [P. 151]
>
> [On arguing with wife] One thing about a hoss—you can always swap her! [P. 87]

> Some folks, when they're drownin', don't mind the wet, just the bad repytation it'll get 'em. [P. 93]
>
> A hoss don't have to talk for hisself very often but when he does he's got two advisers in back and two spokesmen in front. [P. 161]

These stories, arising from the experiences of individuals and told with all the eloquence and ingenuity of gifted storytellers, are not in and of themselves folklore. We define folklore as the part of our culture that is transmitted by unsophisticated means—usually by word of mouth or by example—and has been around long enough, or has become sufficiently pervasive, to be considered traditional. These tales certainly are common enough and were carried in people's memories until they were recorded on paper by the Federal Writers Project fieldworkers, but they remain primarily the possessions of the men who experienced them, not of the culture in general. Frequently stories of this sort become traditional folklore—legends, for example, or jokes. But at this point the tales remain oral histories of fascinating events, about a traditional way of life—horse training.

These stories do hold a mirror up to traditional American activities—not only horse trading but also ways of farming, of approaching a stranger, of addressing a preacher. I suspect that the common thread through these stories of the practical, disapproving, suspicious wife is a motif belonging to folklore and not simply to a few men's experiences and memories. Storytelling too is a traditional activity. Man has always loved stories, and that fascination is still very much alive. My classes in folklore are always curious why people in pioneer years were content to listen to the same tales told over and over, evening after evening. I point out that people today too watch the same stories over and over again every week on television, thus demonstrating that we are no less susceptible to a good story than our grandparents.

In these tales of old-time horse trading, the workers of the Nebraska Federal Writers Project have given us a raft of good stories. They have also preserved a remarkable corpus of rich

21

and unique materials that give us a view of a way of life, now long gone, when a man could, as Lanton Brooks, a horse trader, said in *Foxfire 4,* "tie two or three ol' horses to one good one and take off up the road" (Myra Queen, "Horse Trading," p. 218).

Except where noted, the stories presented here are transcribed verbatim. A few obvious misspellings have been corrected, and punctuation has been altered only where absolutely necessary for the sense. No attempt has been made to regularize the colloquial spelling-pronunciation of words. The few bracketed additions are my own.

Part I: *THE TRADERS*

The Reverend Finmore's
Slightly Excitable Mare

The frontier preacher, or sky pilot, was often courageous and vitally important to the survival of the Plains pioneer community, where the assault on the spirit was often more violent than the physical trials. But just as every other profession on the frontier had its share of questionable practitioners, the clergy too had its shady representatives. Some were not above pulling fancy horse trades or even stealing a team now and then.

The drama of the following encounter is enhanced by the fact that the two protagonists both make their living with their tongue. Here the struggle is not between a master and his dupe but between two masters of their verbal trades. The difference of course is that the preacher usually was presumed to be honorable, ethical, frank, and sincere—a premise accepted in this tale even by Croughan, who should have known better. The road trader, on the other hand, always was presumed to be a no good, lying thief. The result is almost an allegorical morality play, one in which the reader should be well instructed.

This tale, as related by Croughan, is a fine example of some of the strategies used in horse trading: (1) distance, (2) diversion, and (3) back-trading.

As strange as it may seem, the successful horse trader had first and most essentially to appear not *to be interested in trading horses. Imagine that for a moment: the stranger who is clearly in the business of trading horses—trailing a string of horses clearly intended for trading—must seem to be not at all eager to trade them. Indeed, he must feign being not the remotest bit eager even to discuss a trade.*

Croughan remains cool and inadvertently refers to the preacher's horse as a plug. The preacher responds with diversion, implying that he wants to get rid of the horse, of all things, because it is a male horse and he doubts the propriety of his wife—a lady—driving a male horse and so diverts Croughan's attention from the real reasons for his wish to dump the horse. It works: Croughan is so taken aback by this novel tactic that he goes for the trade.

As was often the case, however, both animals have hidden, substantial defects. One of the remarkable features of horse trading was that virtually no horse was perfect to begin with, and as time passed, few horses improved. The only question remaining after each trade was not whether there was a problem but what the problem might be.

In old-time horse trading a truly disastrous horse could be a prize, as we will see in the other tales in this volume (for example, "The Stump Sucker") because the totally useless horse could be the material from which back trades were made. Croughan frequently stuck customers with hopeless horses— and then, once the unfortunate victim learned how truly disastrous his bargain was, Croughan would show up again and offer to reverse the trade, keeping the boot—the extra money or watch or whiskey that had been included in the trade. What is more important, Croughan would not only wind up ahead in the bargain, he would also recover the useless horse and thus the potential for another back-trade further down the road. Indeed, the most valuable horse a roader could have in his string was often his most worthless horse. As Croughan notes later in this text, the trader was always looking for damaged stock that could be fixed up temporarily for a quick and profitable sale, but even better than that was the animal that was so useless that "a good trader could always count on getting back the horse for a song." Almost a fourth of the stories in this corpus carry the theme of the back-trade—for example, the tale of Dinger's mouse-colored mare, "I Just Give Her a Good Whalin' with a Stay Chain," or Joseph Pachunka's tale, "Look That Team Over Pretty Carefully."

In the following tale, collected by Harold Moss on 17 December 1940, Croughan sweetens the chances for a successful back-trade by intimating in the second trading round with the preacher and his wife that the disaster may be even worse than

26

*it appears on the surface: "You never can tell when a horse with
a touch of the asthma is apt to drop dead!"*

Along in the 1890's I was trailing a string of plugs through
northeast Nebraska, looking for trades. Being a pretty industrious trader, I seldom passed up any prospects along the way,
but when I came to a place with a school house squatting in
one corner of the yard, and some ordinary looking farm buildings and a neat white house with green blinds adjoining it on
two sides, I almost decided to pass it up. I never did have any
luck trading with school teachers, especially the school
ma'ams, anyway, and this looked like it might be a school
which had tried to solve a teacher's housing problem by furnishing a complete layout of buildings.

However, I thought better of it and pulled into the yard.
Had I looked closer at the place before, I would have noticed a
rather sanctified, black-frocked devout-looking man sitting on
the little front porch, reading a book, which looked like a Bible.
It was too, and the man turned out to be a preacher of the God-
Bless-You type, who are always bending over backward to do
no evil and rescue their fellow man from sin and iniquity.
Hearing the clatter of the wagon and the tramp of my horses,
he looked up, sort of startled like, and laying down his Bible,
he arose to his full six feet and two inches and marched toward
me, even his undertaker's stride being more or less
sanctimonious.

"Welcome, Brother," he intoned in a sermon-like voice.
"Welcome to God's Acre and A Half and his humble servant's
abode, that of the Reverend Phineas Finmore."

This was going to be an extraordinary experience in trading if we made one, I thought. In fact the whole setup including
the "God's Acre and A Half" was a little fantastic, at least to
me. I returned his greeting with the farmer's "salute" and got
down to the business of the day.

"Reverend Finmore, I am a dealer in better horses and
other chattels and thinking that in some way I could be of
service to you, I took the liberty to call." That was a pretty
high sounding approach for a horse trader, but having had

27

some experience, some not so good either, with preachers and church deacons, I thought it might fit the case a little better.

"God bless you, Brother," he said in organ tones. "I am not exactly a man of horses or earthly things, yet there is in my great work, a material side to be considered and in spreading the gospel there is a need of some of that which is of the earth." It was a neat speech all right, even though he was laying it on a little thick.

It seems, as he informed me, he not only held church in the school house but part of his flock was scattered over the country, which necessitated quite a lot of driving about. He impressed me somehow that he was too wrapped up in his church business to be much a hand at horse trading and it looked like maybe I could even up one of those church deacon deals which hadn't turned out so well. In some ways he sized up as a "babe in the woods" outside of his religious life.

"My good wife, God bless her," he said, "is a devoted soul and carries the message of righteousness and God's comfort to the faithful brothers and sisters." These crusades of his wife, it seemed, required considerable traveling about the neighborhood and beyond.

"Now you," he went on, "as a man of horses, might have the goodness to extend me a bit of helpful advice concerning a slight difficulty we have with the driving horse my wife uses. She is a noble creature"—he meant the horse, not his wife—"but is just a trifle excitable, nothing serious you must understand but still I worry about it."

"Reverend Finmore," I hastened to grab at the opportunity so adroitly presented and which turned out to be a hook, "nothing could give me more pleasure and if you would show me this 'plug,'—I mean mare—perhaps we can find a way out of your difficulties."

He fairly beamed on me as he led me to a little stable and pointed out a very smooth looking, well-proportioned chestnut sorrel mare, who appeared to be sound as a dollar except a few old scars on her heels, but no other blemishes. Of course to a horse man, these heel scars could mean a dozen things, but naturally I thought about kicking. Still, I reasoned, it was

28

hardly likely that his wife would be driving a kicking horse. The mare looked to be about a seven year old, was in good flesh and a nice mover with the halter.

I asked him how she drew and he replied in a voice, throbbing with earnest emotion, "Bless you, Brother, she draws fine and can show a clean pair of heels to many of the drivers around here." I found out one driver she showed them to later, all right.

Then he just stood and eyed me, his finger and thumb tips pressed together, after the manner of a very unctuous gentleman. "And now what do you suggest I do?" he asked after his studied interlude of silence.

"Come," I said, and led him over to my outfit. I had a good old common work and driving horse, a bay, which was smooth-mouthed but not too obsolete and a good molder. "There is a horse you can trust your wife to drive," I told him. "In fact, he is a regular children's horse, gentle as a lamb and easy action; your wife will be perfectly safe with him."

"But," and he hesitated, "would it be proper for my wife to drive a male horse?" He asked this innocently enough but it surprised me somewhat and in fact I had never given such a matter any thought before.

He hurried to justify his rather odd question by stating that he had somehow had an idea that a woman was safer with a mare horse.

"Well," I told him, "I've never heard it mentioned before, and of course my horse isn't a stud anyway." He blinked and recoiled a little, probably because I used the word "stud," and then agreed that it probably wouldn't make any difference after all.

He had me a little confused with his unexpected, somewhat unusual technique and I asked him which kind of rig his wife drove, stalling a little in order to try and figure him out better. He led me over to a low shed and showed me a single buggy, which was well kept and in good condition. It was fitted with a tongue to drive double and he explained that when his wife used it he changed the tongue for shafts, as she drove only single.

Something about that tongue interested me: it had been cracked and was toggled up with baling wire. The left single tree also showed dents and was splintered off in one place. That looked very much like a kicking horse had been around. I didn't see any sign of the shafts and wondered where he kept them, but I didn't ask him. It looked a little suspicious, but I still couldn't bring myself to believe that such an unusual preacher would hold back the truth.

"Would you care to give me your mare and twenty-five dollars for my horse?" I asked him point blank. He pursed his lips and looked thoughtful, then quoted some scripture, and finally said, "Bless you, my brother, the Lord shall guide us in this." Just what he meant I couldn't be sure of, but it sounded all right. Actually, I didn't think that he would do it anyway and was surprised when he suddenly said, this time in a low soft voice, "We are two righteous souls, groping about in a wicked world of material deceit. Would you, my friend, accept my mare and fifteen dollars for your horse?"

Well, we jockeyed around a while and I hung out for twenty-five cash because it was evident that he wanted to get rid of that mare. Finally he admitted that he didn't have twenty-five dollars but that he had a very good watch, which he might work into the deal somehow. He showed it to me and it looked like it was worth something, so we traded.

He told me that his mare was a good driver but he couldn't be sure how she might perform on a wagon, such as I drove, since he had never used her on a wagon.

Once the trade was made, he seemed in a bit of a hurry and busied himself hitching my bay horse up double to the buggy with another bay which he had brought up from the barn. It was a fair match for the one he got from me, but a younger horse. Up to this time I had seen nothing of his wife, but she was around all right and appeared promptly when he called toward the house, "Oh Sister Finmore, we had best drive over to Brother Mullet's for prayer."

She was a small mouse-like woman, swaddled in long, voluminous black skirts which swept the ground.

I was just getting the new mare hitched up to the wagon
to try her out. Brother Finmore seemed all at once to be in a
hell of a hurry to get to Brother Mullet's for prayer. He hustled
his wife into the buggy, which I noticed for the first time had
two broken places in the dashboard, and with a parting "God
bless you, Brother Croughan, and speed you safely on your
way," he wheeled his team toward the road and disappeared in
a cloud of dust.

It took me several minutes to get organized to take the
road again and the preacher and his wife were well out of sight
when I climbed into the wagon and gathered up the lines. I
noticed that my new mare twisted her head around and gave
me a surprised look and laid her ears back. She didn't seem to
like the situation any too well and I kept a close eye on her,
being pretty sure by now that she was a biter and a kicker.

We started moving and she went about three steps and
then with a squeal rammed back against the double tree, lifted
her heels and let go with a wallop that would have knocked
the side out of a barn. It was a beautiful kick at that and if she
hadn't been so good and long range it would have landed in my
middle. As it was she hit the top bow of the wagon and broke it
clean off. This all happened right in the preacher's yard and I
knew now why Brother Finmore was in such a hell of a hurry
to take care of his prayer meeting; he didn't want to be around
when his "slightly excitable" mare started kicking.

I put a trip rope on the mare's right hind leg and ran it
through a pulley, attached to the collar and back to the seat.
Then I started off and when she started the next kick—it
wasn't long in coming—I set her down with a jerk on the trip
rope. After four or five times of that she got tired of trying it.
We jogged along and I wondered if she ever kicked that way
with the preacher and if he knew about a trip rope for kickers.

About two miles and a half up the road from the preacher's
place I came to a farmer's place. There was a team and buggy
hitched to a post in the yard and somehow the rig began to
take on a familiar look. And sure enough, it was the preacher's
outfit with my old plug standing there, his head between his
legs. I guessed this must be Brother Mullet's place and that

most likely, since no one was in sight, Brother Finmore must be deep in his delivered-right-to-your-doorstep prayer service.

An idea struck me: Why not stop and have some fun, maybe make a back-handed trade with Brother Finmore? The mare was acting all right by now and I stopped first and going about it easy, I took off that trip rope, figuring she wouldn't notice it was off and consequently not try any of her lambasting tricks. Then I pulled into the yard and stopped, but didn't get out of the wagon.

For a time there was no sign of anyone or any commotion around. They must be deep in prayer, I reasoned, and so just took it easy. After a bit, from the house, there came a rising crescendo of voices, including a few "Amens" and "God bless you's," the deep organ tones of Brother Finmore furnishing a perfect background for the higher pitched voices of the others. Then they all emerged from the house, shaking hands and everybody talking at once. When they saw my outfit, they stopped short and stared, lost for further words. I broke the ice by calling to Brother Finmore, "Reverend, I just happened to be passing this way and was anxious to know how you liked your new horse, which I recognized tied here in the yard."

He looked a little doubtful at this and seemed uneasy, as did his skirt-swaddled wife. "Brother Mullet," however, was not disturbed in the least and came right on to get a closer look at my outfit. Then the Reverend spoke: "Lord bless us, it's Brother Croughan, the horseman. H-h-h-how," he stammered, "do you like our little horse?"

"Oh, Brother Finmore, she's a jewel, a treasure." In a hearty voice.

He looked relieved, as did his wife, and wanted to know if she had been the "least bit excitable" when I put her on the road. It was just another feeler he put out to learn if she had kicked any. It was funny how tactful and quaint he was in his choice of words in discussing a mean, kicking horse.

"And how, Brother Finmore, do you like the horse you got from me?" I asked, in the most concerned voice I could muster.

"Bless you, Brother Croughan," he replied, "it may be that I hurried too much coming to Brother Mullet's, but somehow

32

while he seems a splendid animal he appeared to tire out quite
easily and wheezed a little."

"Oh, that," I said, "is just a bit of the asthma, though it is
never very bad on a cool cloudy day like this; he really has his
bad spells on hot, sunshiny days; in fact, you never can tell
when a horse with a touch of the asthma is apt to drop dead."

Now I never heard of a horse with the asthma, the nearest
thing to it being a "bull windy," but the preacher didn't know
anything about that either. But the bay he got from me wasn't
a "bull windy," he was just old and a little broken down.

Brother Finmore and his wife were plainly worried now
and Brother Mullet looked skeptical as he raked a grimy
thumbnail through a ten-day growth of stubby whiskers. This
time—and for the first time—Sister Finmore chimed in, "Oh
Mister Horseman, is there any danger we cannot get home
with the horse?" I noticed that she didn't address me as
"Brother."

"Oh no," I reassured her. "Not if you take it slow." She still
wore a worried look. Prospects for a profitable back-trade
loomed bigger and brighter, and I let them stew and fret for a
while.

Finally Brother Finmore said a little timidly this time,
"Bless you, Brother Croughan, would you consider trading
back the little mare for your horse and you keep the watch for
your trouble, and return the fifteen dollars which, I assure you,
I shall put in God's fund, the glory for which shall be bestowed
upon you?"

"No," I told him. "It is bad luck to trade that way and
besides, I'm worried for fear that the little mare might get one
of her 'slightly excitable' spells and hurt one of you."

He seemed to have sensed that I had found out about his
kicking horse and anyway he saw the broken bow on my
wagon. It was certain that he didn't want my old plug and he
made one offer after another until he came down to agreeing
to give me the bay back for the watch and an old mule in my
string, which originally had been black but now was white to
the shoulders. I had even considered giving him away once or
twice. He was skin poor, hide-bound, and a gummer—teeth

33

worn clear down. I could have taken two crooked sticks and a gunny sack and made a mule just like him. On top of it all, he had a spring knee and was blind in one eye.

Finally, after a few dozen more "God bless you's" and quotations from the scripture, he finally told me he would take the mule for my old bay pelter—"to," so he said, "atone for any wickedness which I have been guilty of, though in an innocent way."

We made the change back and as I drove away leading the old bay and still driving his mare, I saw him trying to fit his driving harness to that aged mule. One thing sure, I thought, that mule will never break the pole of the buggy unless he falls over it. I'll never forget how disgusted his own bay horse looked as he was being hitched up with that mule.

Making Camp by a Cornfield

It is easy for people who are dedicated to virtue to differentiate between good and evil, and it is easy for someone who is a full-time, dedicated crook to make such discriminations. But for the horse trader, who lived in the demimonde between respectability and dishonesty, the distinctions were much more subtle. Here, for example, Croughan sees other horse traders stealing corn from the same field in which he is stealing corn; but he is outraged at their thievery, quite accepting his own.

The Federal Writers Project files have no documentation for this tale, but it was obviously told by Lew Croughan and was therefore probably collected by Harold J. Moss during late 1940 or early 1941.

The traveling horse trader, in corn season, always tries to pick up a camp spot near a good cornfield but, at the same time, one not too convenient to a farmer's house.

34

I was in a good corn country in the Elkhorn River territory [of Nebraska], where I picked out a likely looking place along the river by a fine looking field of corn. It was an ideal camp, being handy to water, grass and corn.

I didn't know it then, but around the next turn in the road was another trading outfit consisting of a man, his wife and a lot of kids. He, however, must have known that I was there, considering what happened later. After getting camp set up, I began picking corn. This, of course, was done with the compliments of the farmer, no permission or pay being involved. I had not picked corn for long when I heard voices in the field. At first I thought it might be the farmer, but when I heard a man, woman and two kids hurriedly filling grain sacks with ear corn I wasn't so sure. I figured that no farmer would be husking his corn without a wagon and horses. It looked funny, whoever it was, that they were picking their corn so near my location. If it was another horse trading outfit they would do this in order to throw suspicion on me. So I decided to try a little experimenting by slipping around the field to the other side, where I yelled, "What the hell are you doing there?"

For a few moments with the outfit frozen in their tracks there was a dead silence. Then came a crashing of cornstalks as the gang dropped their filled sacks of corn and ran like scared deer toward the far end of the field. I then gathered up the grain sacks, corn and all, and took them over to my camp. I found plenty of grain to last me for several days. I now wondered what had become of the corn pickers, there being no doubt that they had been helping themselves to someone else's corn.

Early the next morning I broke camp and hit the road. When I rounded the turn to the west of my camp I saw the answer to the cornfield affair. Ahead, about a quarter of a mile, was another horse-trading outfit, still in camp. Half a dozen heads stuck out through the openings of the covered wagon and eyed me uneasily as I approached. A cadaverous looking man straightened up his lanky six-foot figure from a kneeling position in front of a smoky camp fire as I approached. He stared, with a worried expression, at my outfit then relaxed when he was assured that it wasn't a hostile farmer.

I drew up and hailed him: "Howdy, stranger. Just traveling through?" He didn't reply for a space. Then he said, "Yeh, I calculate to hit west. A-goin' to take my woman and kids to the mountains. Old woman's got a distemper." The "Old Woman" now crawled down from the wagon, where she evidently had remained concealed until she got the lay of the land. Holding the folds of a soiled and faded wrapper together across her bosom she made a queer little courtesy [curtsy] then stood and looked at me. Her manner was apologetic and timid. She didn't look very sickly—that is, no more so then most horse traders' women habitually did.

Now, encouraged by their elders, an assortment of stair-step children disengaged themselves from the rickety wagon. In all stages of dress and undress they gathered wide-eyed around my wagon. Several moth-eaten old plugs hobbled around the camp, snatching at the grass and weeds along the way. Damp corncobs lay strewn about, and it was my guess that they had come out of the adjoining cornfield.

Conversation with the man and woman lagged about as quickly as it started, so I prepared to be on my way. They, of course, were the ones I had caught raiding the cornfield, and if it hadn't turned out so funny I would have been pretty hot over what looked like a dirty trick to me; stealing corn near my location in order to make it appear as if I was the guilty party.

"That's a fair looking cornfield over there," I said to them, adding "Crops are sure good around here." The cadaverous trader looked at me a little narrowly and acknowledged that it was.

"You're darned tooting it is," I heatedly replied. "And I calculate to stop at the house up there and see if the farmer will sell me a little feed for my string. Some of these unprincipled scallywags have the gall to go right into a man's fields and take his corn without asking or paying for it."

These remarks inspired the lean horse trader to make some observations himself on the orneriness of such unprincipled skunks. He summed up his statements with "It's a low-down trick and downright dishonest."

If he had had any idea of the surprise in store for him he wouldn't have let himself in for this hypocritical talk. You see, I had his empty grain sacks—they were worth about twenty-five cents a piece—and as I began driving away I tossed them at his feet with the remark, "Take these. Maybe the farmer will be shy of sacks when you stop to buy your corn."

Then with a sober expression on my face I added, "Some careless party went off and left them laying up the road a piece. I'll just give them to you."

The trader's face turned red as a sunset as he recognized his own sacks. I, without another word, drove off.

Slade's Hot Dapple Gray

The source of the following story was Albert Bauer of Lincoln, Nebraska, who was born in 1857 on the present site of Louisville, Nebraska. Harold J. Moss, who collected the tale on 20 May 1940, described him then—at the age of 82—as "really a remarkable character of rugged physique with a deep, booming voice and a twinkle in his eye."

Cass County [Nebraska] in the seventies and eighties was a sort of Paradise for horse thieves. The "hills and hollers" and trails made it easy for them to carry on their business and hide out their horses. One outfit, known as "Slade's Bunch," was the master operator but a few independent scaliwags hung out in the neighborhood around Louisville and did a pretty good business. Of course they were a little chummy and did a bit of horse trading among themselves, mostly with horses from "over the hill."

They ranged over considerable territory posing as horse traders and probably actually came by some of their stock honestly. Then, on account of their far-flung operation, they didn't compete with each other much.

But trouble broke out when one of the little fish worked off a stolen nag on a stranger who drove through their neighborhood. It was in a modern slang "a hot horse" from just over the line in Saunders County. Now the passing trader, for that's what he turned out to be, was headed in that direction but he was smarter than he appeared on the surface. He pulled into Slade's place, who was the master mind in horse collecting around those parts, and talked horses, meantime hinting he might trade. Slade, who made it a point to keep in touch with his brothers of the profession around there, and their operations, evidently had been a little careless, for he had never up to that moment laid eyes on that dapple gray mare, which his caller showed off so proudly while brazenly making the statement that it was a "hoss from Ierway." Just why Slade's neighbor had selected a rather flashy looking nag might only be explained by the fact that it was a dark night when he removed that mare from its Saunders County habitat.

Well, Slade, being anxious to weed out a "hot number" he happened to be holding himself, lost no time in trading it for the dapple gray and the trader moved on. Slade's neighbor a few days later, while prowling around, chanced to drop in on Slade for a little "shop chat" and it was natural enough for him to look over the newest acquisitions to the Slade stables. The surprised visitor stared in amazement when he spotted that dapple gray, and he could well imagine that complications might develop at any moment. As far as Slade was concerned it was no worry to him but he feared that word might get around somehow that the horse in question could be hooked up with his own operations. Biting off a generous chew of "Plough Boy" plug he turned the unexpected situation over in his rather crafty mind.

The result was that he decided to resteal that mare from Slade and get her out of the country by some hook or crook. Not that he wanted the horse back, but he feared the consequences when and if Slade had trouble over the deal. And eventually that was pretty sure to happen since he thought he

38

had perfectly legal ownership and would no doubt parade his new steed around the country, might even use it to pick up a few not so legal.

So he lost no time in putting his plan into action and raided the Slade stables the very next night, leading away the dapple gray, which by this time was becoming more or less accustomed to these nocturnal jaunts. It was, in itself, no mean accomplishment, for Slade knowing only too well the hazards of horse ownership kept his stables well secured and guarded.

From this point on the plot developed complications with amazing rapidity. The self-appointed Robin Hood who acted mostly to do a good deed for Slade as well as himself took the mare by a circuitous route to a ravine back of his place and left her there for the time until he could devise a plan to take her out of the country.

But early next day a group of determined looking men from Saunders County appeared in the neighborhood and called at the Slade place. It was obvious that they had a tip of some sort. They demanded to see his horses and after a heated parley he was forced to submit to their demands.

It was then that he discovered that the dapple gray mare was missing. His early morning callers, however, looked over his stables and showed no further interest in them. They apparently knew what they were looking for and Slade grew thoughtful as they mounted their horses and departed hurriedly in a cloud of dust. Somehow he felt that the dapple gray was involved but he was in a loss to know just how.

His business-like callers began a systematic combing of the neighborhood and finally reached the place of Slade's neighbor. But he saw them coming and hurriedly dispatched his oldest boy to the ravine to get the mare, take her out the back way and turn her loose in the hills beyond their domain.

Thus abandoned, the mare, after orienting herself, departed for Saunders County via Slade's place. The search by this time was losing its impetus and the searching party, having decided that further effort was useless, turned their horses' heads to the west and started home. Before they reached Slade's place, however, the climaxing episode of the whole affair thrust itself upon them. A dapple gray mare extricated herself from a plum thicket along the road and whinnied. They promptly gathered her in and, since it was but a few rods distance, made off for Slade's place. Slade, who was watching, recognized the mare and didn't know whether to demand his horse back or say nothing. He decided upon the latter course for he had begun to work out the crazy quilt pattern of the rather fantastic chain of circumstances.

"No, I never set eyes on that mare before," he said. "She's just a stray I reckon around these parts." The searching party, with suspicion written all over their faces, resumed their journey homeward, while Slade proceeded to do a little investigating on his own hook. He was a fairly good legitimate horse trader and he was good and mad. Not being a too ardent believer in the old adage about there being honor among thieves, especially of the horse variety, he suspected his neighbor and brother in the profession of having a hand in the thing somehow.

That the mare got out of his stable herself and wandered away seemed too remote to be considered. By careful questioning of his neighbor's boys—who were none too talkative—he began to get an inkling of just how the thing might have happened but what he failed to understand thoroughly was that, had those hard-eyed men from Saunders County found that mare in his stables, he might have been decorating one of the few trees around his place. He blamed the itinerant horse trader for most of his troubles and it was long afterward that the full details of the deal came to light during a heated argument with his neighbor over a set of harness, which somehow turned up in the wrong barn.

Dang Fool Deals

Those thieves were indeed lucky not to wind up decorating trees. On the Plains frontier, murder was punishable by a year or so in jail (unless the victim clearly deserved his lot), and anyone who stole another man's wife was adjudged to have ensured his own penalties, but horse thieves were universally hanged—except when they were shot on the run—or worse. Residents of eastern Nebraska had a reputation for sending southern-sympathizing horse thieves from Kansas and Missouri back south by chopping a hole in the Missouri River ice and pushing the thief under. He might reappear several hundred miles downstream, never to steal horses again, or anything else, for that matter.

Even though their crime was not as serious as horse stealing, the bogus traders described in the following narrative were probably lucky to come off with their lives, for if a horse was valuable to the farmer, so was a day's work, and a wasted trip into town might very well take a good day's travel in the 1890s when the events took place. Harold J. Moss collected this tale from Ed Smack of Lincoln, Nebraska, during October of 1940.

At that time [in the 1890s] there were no saloons down that way [in Otoe County, Nebraska] and whenever anyone felt the need for a little stimulant he usually went to Lincoln to get it. Three farmers around the neighborhood set out for Lincoln one day in a spring wagon intending to transact a little business and refresh themselves a little while they were about it, at some of the numerous bars.

The next morning they prepared to make the return trip and feeling pretty jovial and full of fun, they wondered how they might enliven the long, tedious trip back. At College View, where they had left their team and rig, they encountered a professional horse buyer who gave some glowing accounts of his exploits and the fun he had plying his trade.

One of the three, a rather tall and striking figure but ordinarily somewhat quiet and retiring—even a little mournful—became the life of the party then and there. "I'm goin' to have some fun, boys, see if I don't.

Well, they got their rig ready and drove out of town, everybody more or less hilarious, but Thad Martin, the big one, was easily in the most expansive mood.

They hadn't gone far when they met a bewhiskered individual driving a rather nice, smooth-looking team. Since this was in a day when ten or twelve miles took one into a new, strange world, the lone traveler was a complete stranger to the frolic-some trio and vice versa.

"Hello there, neighbor," boomed the normally retiring Thad in a hearty voice. "That's a right smart lookin' team of horses you've got there." The whiskery stranger stared suspiciously at Thad and made no effort to reply for the moment or even stop. But as Thad pulled up and stepped from his vehicle, a trifle unsteadily, the lone driver also pulled up although somewhat reluctantly and mumbled some sort geeting. Martin swaggered over to the man's outfit and began the examination of the team in his most professional manner.

"You want to sell this outfit?" The stranger, now warming up a little, hemmed and hawed and replied, "Wal now, I didn't calculate for to, but mebbe I might if I got my price."

"How much you reckon that'd be?" pursued the dickering Thad.

"Wal now, I've had the refusal of a hundred fifty dollars around [apiece] on that thar team," ventured its owner cautiously, "But I might shade that a little, seein's how I've got a couple of three-year-olds comin' along."

Martin went through all the hocus-pocus of a horse buyer. He looked in their eyes, their mouth and ran his hand over their sleek sides and sturdy legs. He pinched them in the bellies, made them lift their feet up, one at a time, and then stood back and regarded them critically. Then he climbed up into the wagon and reached for the lines. The stranger let him have them, apparently a little dazed by Thad's fast moving inspection and aggressive assumption. By now his partners

42

were becoming interested and looked on intently, though also a little bewildered. That drove the team back and forth at a smart pace, he walked them backward, taking notice of their gait and flexibility. He even unhitched them and put each horse through a number of maneuvers calculated to expose any hidden defects. At last he seemed satisfied and addressing himself to the owner, he voiced his decision with enough volume to almost be heard over in the next township. "I like your outfit. I'll give you two hundred thirty-five dollars for the team."

Their owner's whiskers trembled and vibrated a little as he protested feebly but it was plain to be seen that he was excited and more than pleased over the offer. His team actually wasn't worth one hundred seventy-five dollars.

"Wal, looks like I ought to have a hundred twenty-five around for those horses. Couldn't make it a hundred twenty, could you?"

"All right," said Thad carelessly. "I'll take 'em. You just bring 'em down to Douglas tomorrow and ask for the horse buyer. Anyone can tell you where to find me."

"I'll be thar," said the exuberant owner as he drove hurriedly off lest Martin should change his mind and back out of what the stranger considered a "dang fool deal" for him.

The boys had about fifteen miles to go yet and for the most part of that distance anyone they chanced to meet was pretty sure to be a stranger. Thad's companions, now entering into the spirit of the thing, were just as eager as their ringleader to play horse buyer. They spent the greater part of the day enroute, stopping farmers and even traveling salesmen and negotiating for their horses, offering unheard of prices, testing out the animals and in nearly every case clinching the deal using the same formula of delivery. "Just bring 'em down to Douglas tomorrow and ask for the horse buyers; anybody can tell you."

But when they drew closer to the home zone and began to encounter familiar faces and some neighbors who knew them, they abandoned the sport, knowing full well that they were apt to be mobbed if any deals were made and defaulted on.

43

Eventually the jokesters arrived at their farms, where they intended to lay low until after the day of delivery. It couldn't do to be seen around town when the delighted horse owners arrived to deliver a most amazing assortment of animals—for the most part, nondescript.

And it was well they did, for sure enough the little village saw more horse activity than for a long time previous. Their first victim, the whiskery individual, arrived almost at daylight, leading his two hundred forty dollar team in joyous anticipation of exchanging them for such a sum of ready cash. He canvassed the town, even routing a few out of their beds, asking for the horse buyers who "anybody could direct him to."

But no one knew any such horse buyer and he was puzzled and worried. This time his whiskers trembled but not from the delightful excitement of selling a one hundred twenty-five dollar team for two hundred forty dollars.

Soon other sellers began to arrive, some leading their animals, others driving them hitched to the vehicles, which, in some cases, the "buyers" had agreed to take over for a most substantial additional sum. One by one these later arrivals started a round of inquiry, asking to be directed to the horse buyers, "whom everybody knew." Citizens, hearing of the affair, hurried to the main street, some hopeful that some sort of a circus or horse show had come to town.

Nobody could be found who knew anything about any horse buyers and the three jokesters, being farmers, were, of course, not connected up with the bogus buying. As the day wore on, one by one the disappointed horse owners turned their faces toward home and dejectedly drove away. "Whiskers" himself was last to depart, and as he sadly hoisted himself to the wagon seat he muttered something about "them danged ornery skunks who ought to be skinned alive."

The next day the trio of horse buyers showed up in town, where they, by a little discreet listening in, heard the story of the horse selling debacle. By now, not feeling so hilarious, they kept quiet and enjoyed the joke in silence. No one was the wiser until long after, but sometime later as Thad Martin was making one of his periodical trips to Lincoln, this time alone,

44

he saw approaching him, along the road ahead, a rig and driver who looked familiar—too familiar in fact.

It was the first victim, the one with the facial shrubbery. Fortunately, there was a side road just ahead and Thad did a little quick thinking and whipping up the horses he whirled into the grass grown trail and regardless of the ruts and bumps proceeded to put some distance between him and the owner of the whiskers. He had a feeling that it was just as well, even if he went out of his way a little, to avoid for the time any renewal of his acquaintance with one who might be inclined to harbor a few grudges.

Horseface Kartek's Bull Windy

Itinerant, traveling traders were notorious for their tricks and unreliable honesty (or perhaps it would be better to say, their reliable dishonesty.) If men were cautious and suspicious in dealing in horses with friends, neighbors, relatives, and countrymen, then imagine how automatically everyone must have assumed that the traveling horse dealer was crooked in the extreme, guilty of every disreputable, cynical, immoral, salacious trick in the book, and of course such an assumption was usually accurate.

How refreshing it is then to hear of the farmer victorious and the traveling trader vanquished! And since it is the bested trader who is telling us the story, I think that we can accept it as true, a remarkable statement when one remembers that we are dealing with a roader. The tale was collected from Lew Croughan on 2 December 1940, by Harold J. Moss.

Several tales of this collection deal with bull windies, and most of them deal with jamming sponges or corks up the eversuffering horses's nostrils. The problem was so common and the deception so widely known that the reader can only be surprised that it seems to have worked so often—especially on experienced roaders like Lew Croughan.

Along in the fall of 1898 I had an extra good string of stock; in fact, eight of those horses were the cream of my summer trading. I didn't want to go high hat in the trade business but it looked to me as if I could get on a little higher plane in my business for once. So, leaving my place in charge of my helper, I set out with those eight top animals, prepared to make a killing.

Heading southwest, I made good time and sold one big black sixteen-hundred pound Norman the first day out. The weather held good and there was plenty of forage and, what was better, handy fields just bulging with corn. The third day out, I crossed into Colfax County [Nebraska] and things looked better than ever, good looking farms, rich crops, and a general air of prosperity. Well, sir, a funny thing happened, or at least as far as I was concerned it seemed that way. I hit a low stretch of road with plenty of grass and likely looking cornfield right along side. There was plenty of ditch water and it didn't show much alkali so I decided to make camp in a grassy sweep where the road ditch eased off.

Some eighty rods ahead was an extra good layout of farm buildings, but while I could see them pretty well their occupants couldn't look right down on me, or so I thought. But that farmer must have seen me all right, for just as I was cooking supper, he showed up riding a chestnut sorrel buggy horse. He was a sort of church deacon type. Since I hadn't had time yet to patronize his cornfield his visit didn't bother me any, and in fact I didn't know for sure he was the proprietor of this farm.

However, he introduced himself as such, his name being Kartek. He was certainly friendly, for the average farmer, toward a traveling horse trader. He just sort of sized up as a neighborly sod-buster and I took him as such. Now, most of the professional horse traders never had much respect for the ordinary run of farmers, as far as his trading skill was concerned, and this Kartek, I figured, was just one of the garden variety.

46

Well, he fell all over himself to be agreeable and openly admired my string of horses. He lingered quite a while, inviting me to come up to the house and even suggesting that I get some corn out of his adjacent field for my stock. "Just go in there," he said, "and help yourself. Glad to have you. Like to see good horses like that have some grain."

I was supposed to be a cagey old trader but damned if I didn't go for the innocent-faced, friendly farmer's neighborliness. He was, or so it looked, just a babe in the woods, and even while he lingered there to just visit I was scheming to put over a good trade on him. However, I didn't make the unpardonable blunder of talking trade there by the roadside, or so I thought, since he had extended such a hearty invitation for me to call at his place.

Finally, with a wave of his hand and a congenial smile, he rode away, not however without again reminding me to be sure and stop at his house. He needn't have worried, for I sure had already decided on that. What with his kind invitation to help myself to his corn, I was soon in that field and for once picked corn without worrying about some outraged farmer showing up with a pitchfork. Since he had insisted that I help myself in such a big-handed way I didn't want to offend the old boy by being skimpy, so I didn't stint things in picking about six bushels, ear measure, of that corn.

The next morning I broke camp and pulled my outfit with my string of horses trailing up to Kartek's place. He was right on the job too, with a cheery smile and a warm welcome. "This," I thought, "is going to be good—for me!"

His enthusiasm knew no bounds, or so it appeared. He hurried into the house and immediately reappeared followed by his good wife, who not only carried a youngster in her arms but was trailed by two others, a toddler and a five-year-old. Spying my little dog, who stuck his nose out through the wagon cover, Kartek let out a glad cry and began to make over the dog. He started out on a line of silly "dog talk" and damned if that fool dog wasn't taken in, just like I was, and in a flash he was down on the ground and playing and romping with the biggest kid. Afterward, when I got to thinking it over, I had to take my hat off to that farmer; he sure had a way with him, even to taking in dogs. For that dog didn't ordinarily make friends with anyone that he hadn't been around for some time.

Well, his wife entered right into the spirit of the occasion and almost blushed as she talked baby talk to the brownie she held in her arm: "See the pretty horsies," she cooed to that youngster and "Wave your paddies to the nice man," meaning me. "Regular old-fashioned home folks," I thought, "and just ripe for a good horse trade."

Kartek hustled me right over to the milk house for a drink of buttermilk—a slug of "red eye" would have suited me better—while his wife hurried to the back porch and was back in a flash to feed meat scraps to my dog. Such hospitality I hadn't encountered for a long time, and I almost made a weak vow not to skin my generous host too much if we got to trading. That, I found out later, was entirely unnecessary in view of what Kartek did to me.

He certainly had me lulled to sleep all right and offhand I thought they were just good folksy folks who were just chock full of this neighborly business. His wife stayed right on the job too, even invited me to have dinner with them, while Kartek seemed to have declared a holiday in honor of my visit. He ushered me around, showing me his hogs, chickens, cattle, and equipment, but I noticed that he completely neglected to show me his horses or talk horse, outside of insisting that I turn my string out into a feed yard where there was plenty of water and hay. He showed considerable interest however in a nine-year-old dark brown Norman work-horse which was about the best animal in my string. In fact, it was a better horse than the one I sold, though they matched up good. This horse stood me about a hundred forty dollars and was almost too good for a horse trader to have around.

Well, my trader interest made me anxious and curious to see his stable of horses and after I'd looked over his hogs and chickens and made over them and his kids a bit, I hinted that he must have some pretty fair horses himself. He laughed a little, sort of apologetically, and said, "They're not so much, I'm afraid, neighbor, sized up against yours, but I do have one

48

that's a 'Jo Dandy,' exceptin' that he's a little light for heavy field work. Now that big brown you've got there is just about the kind of a horse I like, but, shucks—you wouldn't deal him to me, I don't suppose."

"Well, friend, I like the cut of your jib and the neighborly way you treat folks," I told him, "and maybe we could deal right free and profitable to both of us."

That seemed to please him and he led me toward the barn, which was a big one and well kept up. His wife, who had set about starting dinner by preparing two fat chickens, appeared again, minus the baby this time, and went along with us making every effort to be sociable and agreeable.

Kartek hadn't done justice to his horses, or so it looked, when he said they couldn't hold a candle to mine. He had a dandy string, and the one he mentioned to me as being a little too light for field work was sure a "pippin" as far as looks were concerned.

He was a "sandstone" bay and was maybe two hundred pounds lighter than my Norman but had good lines, was well proportioned and smooth as velvet. He couldn't have been over an eight-year-old, had all his cups and was a good molder—that's a horse that has near perfect grinder teeth and can mold his feed in good shape; a horse, you know, loses his cups when he is around nine years old and is then known as "smooth-mouthed."

He looked like an all-around horse to me, and no visible blemishes. It was funny in a way and odd horse trading tactics too, for an old trader like me. There we were, each bragging up the other fellow's animal and to a man up a tree it would have looked like one of those "Golden Rule" trades. But it didn't quite turn out that way. That bay of his looked good to me, and the more I saw of him, the better he looked too. We led him out and I walked him around the yard. He had top action and was well gaited too, and not a sign of any defect in his performance.

Kartek wanted my heavier draft horse, but actually seemed modest about his bay and still somewhat apologetic over the whole thing. "Of course, neighbor," he said kind of

49

slow-like, "I wouldn't think of askin' you to swap even. Your horse is better'n mine any which way."

As they stood, I didn't figure more than fifteen dollars difference and seeing that Kartek had been so nice to me, I only planned to try and squeeze thirty dollars boot out of him, though I didn't think that he would give it. I was getting on to dinner time and I never liked to trade on an empty stomach so when he suggested we talk it over after dinner, I was glad to cooperate.

Well, they did things up in grand style and I don't suppose I ever had a finer meal of victuals than the Mrs. set out— plenty of chicken, sweet potatoes, and a lot of other dishes topped off with cake and such like. It was perfect, and Mr. and Mrs. just tried to outdo one another in seeing that I had plenty of everything. It was "Mr. Croughan this" and "Mr. Croughan that"; "Won't you have more of the white meat," "Do have some more chicken, Mr. Croughan," "Pass Mr. Croughan the pickles," and so on until, hearty eater that I was, I had to call a halt. I bragged that dinner to the skies and the Mrs. just blushed and redoubled her efforts to keep me packing it down. She even left the table and rigged up a big dinner for the "nice little doggie," who by this time was in the way of becoming a life-long, do-or-die friend of the Karteks.

The meal finally ended with me privately wishing that there were more nice neighbors and "Golden Rule" folks in the world like the Karteks. It was certainly a revelation in humanity, I thought, and so it was, but not just like I was thinking.

As enjoyable as the occasion was, I was anxious to try and make that swap and be on my way. That dinner must have softened me up still more, for I decided to ask only twenty-five dollars cash boot instead of the thirty dollars I had previously set.

Kartek was certainly in an affable mood and he all but carried me around on a tray. I finally got him headed toward the barn and steered the small talk around to trading. My Norman horse was munching hay contentedly at one of the feeder racks and Kartek eyed him admiringly, then turned to me and clapping me on the back he said in a jovial tone of voice, "Brother Croughan, this horse swap—if we make it—is going to be a gentleman's affair, eh? Now that we know each other and both of us reliable like and open and shut for honest dealin' and no tricks."

I heartily agreed with him and marveled that such a trusting soul was to be found this side of St. Peter's Pearly Gates. He declared that he had no doubts about my horse, adding, "Your word is better than your bond with me." So I told him again just to make it strong that my horse was sound as a dollar and so he was. He looked real pleased at this and murmured a few words about how fine it was that there were at least two people in the world who could trust one another in a horse trade. He did lay it off pretty thick, as occurred to me afterward, but at the time I had a fixed idea that he was just a big hearted sucker and I let down all the bars and eased the way for him to do what he did.

Well, we finally got down to business and he readily agreed to pay me twenty-two dollars and fifty cents cash boot and trade me his bay for my heavey horse. I didn't realize it until afterward but Kartek at no time made any representations about his bay horse. I really wanted his bay anyway because he would match up a bay mare I had pastured out back home.

We made the deal all right and I got ready to set out after rounding up my string including the new horse. You'd have thought from the send-off they gave me that I was a long-lost son or something. The good wife fixed me a lunch to take along and gave my little dog a parting pat on the head as he frisked around her, leaping to lick her hand, and he being a dog that ordinarily was suspicious of all traders at least. He was just as big a sucker as I turned out to be.

As I pulled down the road, trailing my string, Kartek, his wife, and the biggest kid stood in the yard and waved "Goodbyes" until I was practically out of sight. My new horse jogged along easily and the twenty-two dollars and fifty cents jingled in my pocket. I felt pretty good, but not for long. After about three miles or a little better, there was a hell of a commotion at the back end of the wagon—first a loud, wheezy snort, then

51

the ungodly choking, spasmodic sounds of a "bull windy" with his wind clean blocked. They sound just like a bull.

It was that new bay of Kartek's, and he had his head between his legs trying to ease up his breathing and get rid of the pressure. Kartek had plugged his nostrils with sponges to keep his wind down; that was why he hadn't been noisy up to the time. He had blown both those sponges out and I saw them, knotted cords and all, laying in the road. I thought he wouldn't live through it but he did somehow, and then he just stood there and trembled. A horse like that is not worth a tinker's dam to anyone except for trading purposes.

I did a lot of thinking while that bay was getting the kinks out of his breathing apparatus. I might have known that Kartek had something up his sleeve, putting on the play that he did. It was, to use the modern term, a new perfect build-up. The way I figured it, he probably saw me and my string of horses when I made camp that night and he came down to see if I had anything worthwhile that he might turn that "bull-windy" into. My big Norman horse evidently caught his eye, and he did some fast thinking, right on the spot, which resulted in his scheme to get me all softened up and ready for the "kill." He was thorough enough at that, for he played his wife and kids in on the setup to get my confidence. Besides, he turned me loose on his cornfield, but he probably guessed that I'd do that anyway. And the dinner and the whole-souled friendliness and his remarks about the gentleman's horse trade. He sure made a sap out of me. He did me in for about one hundred and fifteen dollars on that deal, and I had a good mind to go back and raid his cornfield again at least, but decided against that. He probably wouldn't have been so all-fired friendly the next time.

I made camp early that night, on account of that "bull windy" bay horse mostly. A farmerish looking fellow who turned out to be a country lawyer drove by in a phaeton and stopped a minute to look me over. He studied that bay horse for a minute or so and said to me, "You didn't by any chance come by that horse down to 'Honeyface' Kartek's, did you?"

I admitted that I had.

"Well," he said, "You're lucky you got your shirt left. That Kartek's about the slickest proposition around these parts. That's why they call him 'Honeyface,' because that fellow can skin you in such a nice neighborly way. He bought that horse for a ten-dollar bill, I know positive. But maybe he didn't get much out of you. I take it you're a professional trader."

"Well, he got plenty," I told him. "In fact, he got my best horse and maybe I'm not so damned professional after all." Then I give him an account of the whole deal, and he drove off, laughing fit to kill, and with a few noisy whoops and wows thrown in. "That's 'Honeyface' to a TYT," he called back.

It wasn't much consolation to me that Kartek was such a genius at trading but it was all water under the bridge and I quit worrying and made up my mind to work that "bull windy" bay off of the first man I met, and who was "workable." For a good-looking young horse still "in his cups" that "bull windy" was about the worst "white elephant" I ever got a hold of. He couldn't navigate much over a mile without choking on his own wind and we had to move along at a snail's pace. I tried out two prospects but they shied off and wouldn't even consider any kind of a deal. Completely disgusted with both myself and that bay horse, I'd just about made up my mind to give him away to the first person who would take him.

Moving along slowly I finally came to a sort of four corners combination blacksmith shop, store, post office, and what-have-you. The proprietor, a big strapping Bohemian, was standing out in front of his place, holding a mail sack in one hand and a blacksmith's leather apron in the other. Whether or not he was shifting the theater of his activities from the blacksmith shop to the post office or vice versa I couldn't quite make out, but it proved to be the latter, and he headed toward the lean-to shop adjusting his leather apron as he went. However, he was all eyes for my outfit and stopped short of his shop entrance to gawk.

I pulled up and hailed him with that sweeping, friendly salute so familiar to farmers and others of the horse-rig days on the open road. He returned the salute, but without much enthusiasm. He spoke a studied, painstakingly correct English such as some of the European peoples affect and asked me, "Would I care to draw up and rest a bit."

The name "Demus" was crudely lettered on one of the store windows and I naturally concluded it must be his. When I hove into sight there wasn't a person in sight except Demus, but by the time I had stepped down from the wagon, three or four tacky looking denim-clad individuals appeared out of nowhere and surrounded my outfit, gaping and gestulating somewhat excited. They were talking Bohemian evidently, but I couldn't understand a word they were saying. Well, to make a long story short, I soon had Demus interested in my string and he admitted he might be on tap for a deal. It seemed he was a man of many sides and dabbled in farming along with his shop, store and post office

The "bull windy" bay was standing quiet and breathing regular, so he looked to be in his usual splendid form. I had to work fast with Demus or not at all, I figured, so I just laid my cards on the table and told him I had too many horses and seeing I didn't have a match for the bay (and I didn't either; in fact, I doubt if one existed—that is, such a good-looking "bull windy!"), so I would sell him outright for a third of his worth.

"That," I told him, "would be about fifty dollars."

Demus, I could see, was getting the fever and showed it strong, in his eyes and actions, and I began to feel pretty good at the prospects of unloading that "bull windy" on him. I left the bay on his rope, for I couldn't afford to leave any handy opening for Demus to try out the horse on the road and show up his defect. Anyway, I had his nostrils plugged up with the sponges Kartek had fixed him up with.

He finally offered me forty-five dollars, and after a faint protest I agreed to take it. Then the unexpected had to happen. One of those hangers-on, a big harmless looking, over-grown lout drew Demus aside and talked to him in Bohemian. Demus listened a while and nodded his head. Then he turned to me and said, "My friend, I would like very much to take your horse a few steps up and down the road to just see him work a little."

I couldn't refuse without arousing suspicion on his part, so reluctantly I agreed, meanwhile praying the bay wouldn't go

54

into one of his "bull windy" spells. But those few steps turned out more like miles than steps, and that damned horse blew the plugs, choked up as usual, and got noisy.

I still don't believe Demus knew what a "bull windy" horse was, but he did know that there was plenty wrong. He shook his head when we finally got the bay back and straightened out in his breathing, and said slowly and carefully, "I am afraid very much that I cannot use your horse." Then he seemed to reconsider and finally he added, "But I will give you ten dollars for him."

I took the money. In fact, I think I would have left the horse with him anyway if he'd let me. It was all in the game and I had thirty-two dollars and fifty cents to show for my one hundred and forty dollar Norman draft horse. I couldn't be sure but I thought that that meddlesome hanger-on had probably recognized the bay "bull windy"; more than likely he knew Kartek, who didn't live so far away at that, and of course also knew that the bay horse was no good in wind. I wondered what Demus intended to do with the ten-dollar animal and decided that maybe he was smarter than I thought and would figure on skinning some other sucker with the bay, which was probably just what he did.

I Pulled Out to See a Little More of Arkansas

On 1 May 1940, Lew Croughan related to Harold Moss a long narrative about a trip he had made to Arkansas in 1898.

There were probably plenty of other places more favorable to profitable trading but I sort of enjoyed traveling through odd and out-of-the-way places and being more or less footloose and fancy free, as were most horse traders. I had a desire to see what Arkansas looked like.

55

With a few cheap burros, a couple of mules, a saddle horse and one good wagon team I pulled into the rough Ozark section of western Arkansas. What they called a road was just a boulder-strewn hollow and the going was rough and slow. The mosquitos, ticks and chiggers were just plain hell and I began to wonder whether or not this Arkansas jaunt was a smart thing or just a fool-killing venture. There hadn't been even a pretense of a house or humans for some three or more miles. Nobody apparently did much traveling on that rocky course. It looked like a hell of a place for a horse trader to come to, all right.

I didn't see the little log cabin until I was right on top of it. Then it might have remained unnoticed but for the combined barks and yaps of half a dozen assorted skin-poor dogs. The cabin looked deserted—that is, until the dogs had kept up their racket for a space. Then all at once about a dozen heads stuck out of the burlap curtained windows and door and the cabin just bristled with human occupants. A lanky, listless man and a scrawny, tired-looking woman appeared in the door, stared at my outfit a full minute, and then cautiously left the shelter of their barren quarters and advanced a few shuffling steps toward the wagon. The road—what there was of it—ran right through the edge of the clearing around the house, and I had pulled up, though just a bit uncertain as to how one approached these simple mountain folk.

The man and woman resembled one another to such a degree that I half way thought that they were brother and sister. You see, I wasn't entirely familiar with the fact that a lot of those Arkansas hill people looked alike anyway, and on top of that there was a lot of inbreeding or intermarriage of relatives. To be more explicit, they run their stock down to the point where they had the same general, dead-pan appearance. Back in those days lots of the hill people down there rarely traveled any distance from their home base and so the only folks they ever met were mostly relatives.

I hailed the two, without getting down from the wagon, but neither one of them uttered a word. They just stared at the canvas-covered wagon. The man gulped and drew his claw-like

56

hand across his eyes just as if they were playing tricks on him. Slowly they advanced, still staring. Finally the stringy-looking man broke the silence: "Son, what you-all got there. Is that your cabin?" It was my covered wagon that had them flabbergasted. They had never seen such a thing before.

Those people finally ventured up close enough to touch the wagon. They poked at its canvas top and peered under it to see what was inside. Suddenly, as if struck by an idea, that "billy" turned to the woman and said, "Jezibel, you-all get the young-uns out here."

The "young-uns" must have been sharp-eared, for at that they came pouring out of that windowless cabin, all sizes and ages from toddlers to eighteen-year-olds. One of the biggest girls was carrying an infant, practically naked, much like she would have handled a sack of meal. As near as I could count there was about a dozen kids all together, most of them half to three-quarters naked. The older girls, who were not bad looking, clutched their ragged, faded calico dresses tight about their forms so as if to conceal numerous rents and holes in the cloth and which revealed patches of naked skin underneath. They wore no underwear, shoes, or stockings, and they seemed to feel somewhat ashamed of their semi-naked state—with their well developed breasts almost entirely exposed, their hair uncombed, and bodies unwashed. Their ragged dresses were the button-down-the-front style, only the buttons were completely lacking.

That gang swarmed around the wagon wide-eyed and mouths agape. The half a dozen dogs, encouraged by the presence of the family, mingled with the crowd and sniffed at the wagon wheels, delighted no doubt to find a little variety of life aside from the same old trees and posts.

"Dabney"—that was the man's name—wanted to know about the wagon, didn't even know the names of any towns over ten miles away. I asked them where they went to school but the kids just looked blank. The woman however guessed that there was a school house somewhere down in "Magazine Holler," but they had never been down in that country.

There was plenty grass and water around, so I decided to make camp. They were tickled pink and the whole gang hustled around to help me get settled. A squad of kids hurried out into the woods and came back with a bucket of blackberries, two of the others grabbed fish poles and hustled down to a little rocky stream. In no time they were back with half a dozen fish. Living sure was made to order around there.

They wanted to get up in the wagon and were sure tickled when I told them to go ahead. I always carried quite a stock of canned goods—salmon, corn, etc.—and I offered them a few cans. Damned if they knew what it was—drew back kind of scared. After I opened one, they just fell over themselves to try the contents—peas, I think it was.

While they were looking over the wagon, I pulled out my plug and took a chew of tobacco. Two of the older girls, one of them by now half out of her skimpy dress, watched me closely and with much interest. A little later one of them came up to me, stuck her finger into her mouth, and said, "Mister, would you-all give me a piece of that 'store terbaccer? This here long green makes my mouth sore as hell!"

I give her a whole plug and she bit off a chunk big enough to choke a horse and then passed it around to the other kids. As near as I could make out, every kid took a chew except the two toddlers, and they kept begging for it.

Just before supper Dabney's old woman came out to the wagon with a plate of soggy corn pone and a slice of razor-back sowbelly. The stuff didn't just exactly whip up my appetite, but a few minutes later, when she showed up with a jug, I commenced to get interested. She said it was "wine" and would I accept of it. Would I? Well, you'd only need one guess to answer that one!

Since she called it "wine" I naturally thought the stuff couldn't have much power, so when I tipped that jug up I let about half a quart of it slide down before I came up for air. She stood watching me, a half grin on her shallow face. It was funny tasting but mighty good and I started to hit it again.

58

"You'd better hold off a little while, Son." She looked worried as she said it. "That thar's liable to bog you down. It's a heap strong."

She wasn't fooling either, for I went out like a light right after supper. Just managed to crawl up into the wagon and flop.

She called it "wine," but it must have been something new in that line. The next morning I was still groggy but another drink—not so hog-size that time—brought me around fine and ready for a most interesting day. Before I left, Dabney told me it was made out of blackberries, corn, dandelions and some other ingredients, cooked and run in "middlin's"—whatever that was [the main run from a still]—what a hell of a mixture. But it sure was good. I traded them a plug of tobacco for another gallon of the stuff. They wouldn't take money—said they had no use for it.

Well, the next morning, after I got rid of that hangover, I began to make preparations to leave. There didn't seem to be any prospects of a trade around there. Dabney just had one broken-down mule and no money. The whole outfit gathered around the wagon and didn't look any too cheerful. They acted like they hated to see me leave. Finally, Dabney said to me, "Mister Croughan, don't reckon you-all could stay another sun, could you? It sure would make us all God-almighty happy if you would. Thar's goin' to be a few folks around to see your wagon; none of them never seen anything like it."

How in hell anyone knew I was there was beyond me. No one had passed that way I knew of, but it must have been that some of Dabney's children had slipped away the night before while I was "under the table," and spread the news. Pretty soon they started trickling in, some driving mules, but most of them afoot. It was a regular field day for them and my covered wagon was the center of interest. One old scrawny "billy" said he had come five "mounting" miles—he meant over the hog backs—and that was about as far as he had ever ventured away from home before.

One of those thin, hide-bound fellows—the whole crowd was gangling scrawny—had a slow mule and after a lot of persuading he agreed to swap it for one of mine and give me two and a half dollars to boot. I don't know yet why, because mine was as worthless as his. The trouble was that he couldn't raise the two-fifty boot in the whole crowd. They didn't have any money or any use for it, I guess. He finally managed to get a hold of a dollar and thirty cents. Then he offered me a gallon of straight corn liquor—he must have brought it with him— and we made the trade. After a bit, they got to squinting at the sun and pretty soon the whole caboodle of them straggled off to wherever they lived.

My friends gave me a fitting send-off and I pulled out to see a little more of Arkansas. I came damn near seeing it double, what with my ever growing stock of "Mountain dew." Everywhere I struck a trade I got one or two gallons more of liquor. It wasn't worth much down there, so I held onto most of it, except the few gallons I felt the need of in transit.

Back in Nebraska, with twelve jugs of Arkansas moonshine, for once I was in a position to deal in something besides horses. I was flying with the geese while the stock held out, and sure softened up some tough prospects with that Arkansas mountain dew.

New-fangled Farming

In the following tale we have a classic example of narrative skills in the folk mouth. The story opens with an attention getting line worthy of Twain, and the detailing is as subtle and accomplished as the prose of any professional writer.

Early humorous American phonograph records, some surviving old-time storytellers still seen on television (Grandpa Jones or Junior Sample, for example), and preserved narratives like these horse-trading stories were considered to be funny in their content and style, not because of a punch line. As a result, many of the earlier tale forms are much longer than we are accustomed to in the 1980s (when a joke may well consist of a punch line alone), and the expected punch line simply is not there.

The power of this following story is in its flow, the events described, and the details of the transaction and experience—for example, the motif of the farm dogs loafing in the yard and being kicked out of the visitor's path as a gesture of hospitality!

Croughan obviously would have sympathized with Earl Conrad's father, who said, "Every other man in town's got a broken wrist from crankin' them damn Fords. I'd rather get kicked by a hoss than a crank" (Horse Trader, pp. 45–46).

"Hi, you horse trader! Buyin' anything today? I mean for cash?"

I hadn't noticed the fellow before but there he was, his khaki pants and shirt sort of blending into the heat-seared, grass-covered earth. In the background was a collection of unpainted, weather-beaten buildings, such as one sees in the wheat country of Western Nebraska. Three tractors, their nearly new paint gleaming in the bright sunlight, lent an odd, incongruous contrast to the rest of the surroundings. The speaker, despite his week's growth of dirty black beard, had a cocksure air about him as he, with a swaggering gait, approached my outfit, now halted in the wind-swept road. I hadn't intended stopping at his place, up to now, but the sight of those new tractors gave me an idea, since that was about the time the machine craze was starting to sweep the country.

"I say, trader," he continued with obvious self-importance, "I've got fifteen head of good, sound work horses, worth a hundred dollars around [apiece], and I'm going to let 'em go for twenty-five dollars a head. I don't need 'em anymore. You interested?"

"Well, friend,"—I studied him as I spoke—"horses right now are, just as you say, not needed by anybody much. I don't need 'em any more. But maybe you might let me see them."

He led the way into his machinery-cluttered yard, kicking a couple of mongrel dogs out of the way and indicating an open space which somehow wasn't taken up with farm tools and automobiles. "There's part of 'em right out behind the barn."

61

He made a sweeping gesture to include about ten head of as pretty a bunch of horses as you could find anywhere on a wheat farm. And they were just as good as they looked too. Seven to ten years old, averaging around fourteen hundred pounds and hardly a blemish outside of a few wire cuts.

The owner—his name was Luther—wasn't as old as I first thought and he gave me to understand that he had young, modern ideas about power farming and the obsoleteness of horses. "Yes, trader," he said in a fatherly tone of voice, "the day of the horse is done for us progressive farmers. I've got eight hundred acres of wheat goin' into head right now and it'll make thirty bushels if it makes a peck." And it looked it too, as near as I could tell from a distance, though a lot could happen to a wheat crop between then and harvest.

Well, I bought that ten head, easy as pie, for twenty dollars around and paid him cash, the total being not much more than one head was worth. He seemed tickled as a kid with a new toy and helped me tie in his string with mine, even throwing in the rope halters and ten sets of fair harness for fifty dollars extra. As I started on my way he remarked that it sure was fine to think of getting rid of a big feed bill and a lot of drudgery, taking care of those out-moded horses.

I hit back east shortly after that and though I intended to sell those horses in Sioux City, I only had four left when I reached there. Those ten averaged me eighty-five dollars profit each.

Along in August I drifted out that way again with a string of ordinary plugs which had come out of my summer's trading. These I mostly traded down to a string which was even more inferior. Several times that summer I had wondered how wheat-farmer Luther was making it with his new tractors and modern ideas. Eventually I worked into his vicinity, altering my course slightly to get there, since I was a little curious as to how he was making out. The country looked dry and no mistake, but what was more significant there were several fields of flattened out, reddish brown wheat, which had never been harvested.

62

Making camp for the night just about a mile from Luther's place and near to a sink-hole which still showed in between its mud bumps a thin sheet of grayish water, I set about tending my stock and preparing supper. The early western Plains twilight quickly faded into darkness and lights glowed feebly from the windows of Luther's dwelling. Traveling, as I happened to be, alone, it was not my intention to call on him until the next day. By now a thick blanket of darkness had settled down and the campfire cast up a dull glow. A racket and rattle up the road, in the direction of Luther's place, attracted my attention and, looking up that way, I saw the twin yellow lights of a car bouncing along the uneven surface of the dusty trail.

With a roar and shuddering vibration the car came on, until directly abreast of my outfit, then with a final outburst it stopped abruptly, much like it had struck a stone wall. It was a touring car, with the top down, and its occupant lost no time in extricating himself from the interior and stepping over the low side-door, which as you may recall on those first cars was no door at all, just an imitation with no hinges—though they did have a dummy handle on them.

Being in the firelight I couldn't make out my visitor and he had the advantage of being able to get a firelight view of me. "Well, if it ain't 'trader' himself, or is it?" he exclaimed and asked. "I seen your fire a-burnin' and thought maybe it was another wheat field startin'." It was Luther all right, but somehow or other even in the outer fringe of firelight and darkness he didn't seem quite the "big operator" his attitude the previous spring had suggested.

After an exchange of small talk I asked him how everything was with him. For almost a full minute he was silent, just stood there, as if trying to forget an unpleasant phase of his life. Then he said soberly, "Croughan, things didn't turn out so good for me after all. Since you was here, we had one of those burnin' electric winds and my wheat crop went up the spout. There's a field of it over there, an' I never even cut it. I couldn't pay off any of my machinery and they came and got most of it, includin' the tractors. The worst of it is too that I

63

was damned fool enough to give away all my horses but three. Now I can't even do the fall plowing."

He certainly was right out and out about it and it made me wonder how many other farmers had found themselves in the same boat. Well, we talked along about this and that, but his mind was centered on his troubles and he kept reverting to the subject. After an interval of studied silence he turned to me and, a little jerkily, he put out a feeler: "Croughan"—he had dropped that "trader" business—"I was kinda thinkin', maybe you could help me outa this mess. I need horses now or I can't make a crop next Spring."

"How," I asked, "could I help you?"

Seemingly encouraged he continued, "Would you fix me out with ten head of horses and wait for your money till I make that crop? Nobody around here will stake me. Anyway, most of them were just as crazy as I was and right now they're runnin' in circles tryin' to get just what I am—enough horses to do their farmin'."

It was something new to me and would have been to any roader trading horses. Luther wasn't a bad sort but a man who would throw away his old shoes before he had any assurance that he could hang onto his new ones was none too promising as a credit risk. Still, I thought, his foolishness was the means of making me near a thousand dollars. So I decided to try him out once. However, it was ten to one that he'd never make good on it. He almost fell on my neck when I told him I'd do it and would be up to his place next morning.

The next morning early I broke camp and headed toward his layout. He was out watching me come and met me at the road to escort my outfit into his yard. A guide was hardly necessary though, I noted, for the yard was nearly empty—no bright painted tractors and very little machinery occupied its space now, only two cur dogs lay sprawled out in the driveway, they at least having escaped the "writ of execution" servers. Somehow or other it gave me the curious feeling that those dogs had not moved from their spot all that long summer. Since there was nothing else Luther could do by way of a hospitable

64

gesture, he again kicked those dogs out of the way though I could easily have driven by them.

My horses wouldn't have taken any blue ribbons at a horse show but they could do a lot more work than no horses at all and I let him take nine, all the odd ones I had outside of my driving team and a small driving mare. Besides, I let him have three sets of harness. The price was to be thirty dollars a head. It left me without trading stock, but I had twenty-two watches, the result of a lot of previous trades and these later, with a little extra cash, were the means of my acquiring eight plugs. A horse trader without horses is pretty much like a jewelry store without watches, though a trader has the best of it there—he can handle watches but a jeweler can hardly deal in horses.

Luther invited me to stay on for dinner, which I declined, and as I wheeled out of the yard he kept calling, "Don't you worry, Mr. Croughan"—it was "Mr." now—"I'll pay you come next harvest."

The following August he made his word good and mailed me a check—a good one too—for two hundred eighty-six dollars and twenty cents, the price of the nine horses plus six percent interest.

Elmore Walker's Ramble on the Plains

Often the Federal Writers Project fieldworkers, who did not enjoy such modern reporting conveniences as the tape recorder, simply could not take the time and work to write down anything more than the bare bones of an account. We are fortunate in the following narrative however, collected from Elmore Walker, by James Campbell during the week of 15–22 May 1941, to have plenty of detail about the life of the traveling trader, as well as interesting clues to the situation of the immigrant homesteaders who saturated the northern Plains states during the last three decades of the nineteenth century.

There is good reason to believe that the "Russians" encountered by Walker were not Russians at all but "Rooshens"— Germans from the Volga River and Black Sea areas of Russia. They left the German colonies in Russia during the late nineteenth and early twentieth centuries and settled in large numbers in Kansas, Nebraska, and the Dakotas at precisely the time of this narrative. Although they had lived as colonists in Russia for a full century, they remained culturally and linguistically German, which would explain the apparent similarity here of the "Russian" dialect forms to German. Moreover, the German-Russians were profoundly suspicious of all non-German-Russians, and the unwillingness here to provide even the simplest information to the innocent travelers is typical.

The travels described in the following story are long. Genoa, Nebraska, lies on the Loup River in the central part of the state while Norton County, Kansas, is in the west, several hundred miles distant. The Cherokee Strip is south, approximately two hundred miles from Norton County, in Oklahoma. It is that piece of land lying between the original southern border of Kansas and the corrected border established by a later survey. The Strip was opened for homesteaders on 16 September 1893. The return trip, by way of Wichita, is an additional four to five hundred miles, for a total trip on horseback of nearly a thousand miles.

I'm going to tell you a horse trading story but it is a long one. It covers a trip from Genoa, Nebraska, to Norton County, Kansas, then to the opening of the Cherokee Strip [to white settlers] and back to Genoa by way of Wichita, Kansas.

I and Charlie, my brother, started from Genoa, Nebraska, and went by train to Norton County, Kansas, to our father's home, where we had left our outfit. We took a string of horses and mules mixed. Put Charlie's big bay team his uncle had given him on the tongue of the covered wagon and started for the opening of the Cherokee Strip in September, 1893.

We were just swapping and went to see the race. On our way we crossed the [Arkansas?] River and came into a Russian settlement and for a half of a day tried to find out from them where Alberta was located. We would ask these Russians and they would say, "No forstand English." We finally got tired of it. Charlie said, "The next fellow we ask will either talk or fight."

One of them came along and Charlie said, "Can you tell us where to find Alberta?"

He said, "No forstand English."

Charlie said, "You will talk or I'll whip you."

The Russian said, "Right down over the hill."

Then Charlie asked him, "Why don't you fellows talk?"

He replied, "If we no talk with people, we no can quarrel."

A little further on I went into a place where they had a fine lot of watermelons. I asked a woman if I could buy a melon. She said, "No forstand English."

I pulled a quarter out of my pocket and said, "Hell, woman, I can pay you for it. I don't want it for nothing."

She said, "Three for twenty-five cents."

I handed her the quarter and she said, "Take your pick." I took two striped Rattlesnake melons that would weigh about twenty-five pounds apiece. She said, "Them ain't big enough," so she got me Cuban Queen melons that would weigh about six pounds apiece and said, "I'll get you another."

I said, "Why didn't you sell me a melon before?"

She said, "Big company from city shipped us in here. American, he no like it. People come along, want to buy melon, put melons in buggy, and say 'you got plenty melons' and don't pay for them. When I saw your money, I know you pay."

Right south of Hutchinson, Kansas, about ten miles, we met a man with a spring wagon load of peaches in half bushel crates. We stopped and asked him if he would sell us some peaches. He said, no, he had them for the "uppers" in Hutchinson. "I have all these sold. My farm is just about four miles straight south of here. When you get there, jump out and go in. You will know the place. There is a big orchard. Take all the peaches you want."

I took a bucket and went in and told the woman. She said, "Just go down and help yourself. Get all you want. Go down to the east end of the orchard and get the Red Indian peaches. They are like these." They were a red, rosy peach.

He had ploughed the orchard and throwed the dirt to the trees and left a dead furrow between each row and the furrows were just full of peaches, where they had fell and rolled off. There was a big bunch of hogs. I don't know how many. Hogs everywhere. They would say "woof!" and away they would go. When they got up they would look just like they had come out of the creek. They were so wet with the juice. I never saw so many peaches in my life.

I found the Red Indian peaches they had told me to get. You could just take hold of the stem and pull them apart and the stone would fall out. They were just right to eat. The man was making his living raising peaches and hogs. Quite different from the Russians who had been sent out from the city by a mortgage and loan company and gave them just enough to furnish them a start.

We made a few trades long and finally landed in Hunnewell, Kansas, in the line of the Strip. We followed the line of the Strip down to Arkansas City, Kansas, and made a few trades and saw the races.

My father and half-brother Bill were in the race with a team and rig made from two wheels of a wagon. Dad said, "After we got out about forty miles we found some one there ahead of us."

When the excitement was over we started back to Genoa and came by way of Wichita, Kansas. There was a feed barn on the right side of the street in Wichita. On the barn was a sign, "We buy, sell, and trade horses." When we got in front of the barn a fellow ran out and said, "Say, fellow, will you trade those little black mules for a young team of big gray horses?"

The mules were coming four and five. I said, "All right. All it takes is just to see alike."

He said, "Come in and look the horses over." One was twelve hundred pounds and smooth mouth; the other was five coming six and weighed about fourteen hundred pounds. I

68

wanted him. He was a dead match for one my brother-in-law, Henry, at Genoa had. I thought I would put him in shape on the trip, get him broke, and Henry would give me a hundred fifty dollars for him.

The horse looked at me the same as to say he didn't like me and didn't care whether I liked him or not. I walked out of the stable and started to go back out to the wagon. The feller says, "You didn't say how you was going to trade."

I said, "There would be no use. There is too much difference."

He say, "It never made me mad for a feller to tell me how much, anyway."

"Well," I said, "it will take just twenty dollars to make the trade."

He just pulled out his pocket book and handed me the money and said, "We've traded horses."

I told him to lead out his team and I unhitched the mules from the hind end of the wagon. I handed him the mules' rope and took the horses' rope. I tied the old horse on to the wagon and started to tie the young horse. The policeman stepped up to me and said, "Young man, you can't tie that horse on to the wagon for he will kill somebody."

"Can I hitch him and drive him out then?"

He said, "No. He has tore up enough wagons in this town."

I says, "Then can I ride him out."

He said, "Do you think you can ride him?"

I said, "If I can't, he's the horse I've been looking for several years. I'd like to see the color of the horse's hair that I can't ride."

And he said, "If you'll keep him off the sidewalk you can ride him out."

I said, "Well, I always ride with a braided quirt and if I see I can't keep him off the sidewalk I'll knock him down."

He said, "Fair enough. Ride him out."

I think he wanted to see the fun too.

I pulled my sixty-five pound saddle and my bridle out of the wagon and put the bridle on him. Charlie throwed his coat over his head and I strapped the saddle on him and cinched it up. Then I climbed onto him. Charlie let him go. He commenced to bawl and to buck and run down the street the way I wanted him to go. Every time he would get close to the sidewalk I would double the quirt and hit him over the nose and he would turn quartering across the street. When he got to the other side I would hit him on the other side and turn him back. That is the way I rode him out of town. There were three or four policemen on each side of the street saying, "Stay with him, young feller."

When he quit bucking I got off and a couple of police came up where I was. They told me to take him clear out of the country, for everybody that came along they traded him for a pretty fair horse, then they would get him back for an old skin that would just pull the wagon out of town.

I waited for Charlie to come up. I told the police I wanted to take him to central Nebraska, that my brother-in-law had a horse you couldn't tell from him, the same age. I could get a good price out of him to mate. I intended to quiet him down on the way. When Charlie got there I got on him and rode him to camp.

The next morning we was going to drive him. We harnessed him up and let him up beside the tongue. Charlie was holding him. I stooped down to pick up the neck yoke. He struck me with both front feet. I was close to him and he struck me with his knees as he came up and set me down backwards and came right at me with his mouth open. I hit him on the head with the neck yoke with both hands before I could raise up and knocked him down. He stretched out and Charlie says, "You've killed him."

I said, "I'd rather it would be him than me if it had to be one of us."

He laid there about two minutes, got up, and stepped right up side of the tongue. We hitched right up and drove him to Genoa, Nebraska.

Every town we got into between Wichita and Superior, Kansas, there was a man with a good fair horse jumped us to trade horses. They always picked that horse, but we had better horses in the outfit. At every town there was always a different man sent by them fellers in Wichita to try and trade for the horse. He was a good trading stock for them.

I didn't know then what I had done or I would have let him back. When I hit him I had the misfortune to hit him with the iron on the neck yoke which holds the ring of the neck yoke. I hit him on the joint that holds the neck and caused a poleval. I am a lover of horses and he is the only horse I ever hurt in my life. By the time I got to Genoa it broke and was running.

Henry Harris told me if I could cure it up that there was a man in Genoa buying horses to ship to Texas. (He was a barber. I don't know what his name was. Maybe Shrigley.) He had been wanting to trade him a team of colts, a set of harness and a top buggy for his horse. So I just took a piece of blue vitriol about the size of a bean and a chicken quill and shoved it down into the pipe [that is, the core of the boil], and in about three days I took a pair of nippers and pulled the pipe out. And it healed right over. Combed the mane over it so he couldn't see the scar.

Then on Saturday we hitched him up to the wagon with the mate to Henry's horse. My sister Ida, Henry and I took the eggs and butter and drove to Genoa the same as we always did with Henry's team. We stopped in front of Mullin's Store. Henry got out to help my sister out and took the produce in.

When Henry came out of the store the barber was looking the horse over. He says, "Are you going to trade me this horse today?"

Henry says, "Are you sure you want him?"

He said, "Bad enough to give you that team of colts, a set of harness and buggy for him."

Henry told him to get right into the wagon and we would help hitch the colts and change them. Henry lived east of town and the barber kept his horses in a pasture on the John Lawson place just south of there. The barber kept a man to look after his horses and he lived in a tenant house at Lawsons'. We went past Henry's place; the pasture was half a mile further on. Henry stopped at his house and got another horse. We hitched the colts up and turned the horse in the pasture, got the harness and tied the buggy on behind, left them at Henry's and drove back into Genoa with the barber.

About a week afterwards his man was looking after the horses and told the barber he would have to come and get that horse, that he couldn't get his head to the ground to eat and was eating all the willows in the pasture. The barber hired the veterinary, John Rester of Genoa, to cure him. When he got him cured the price was more than the horse was worth and he give him the horse. Rester used him for a single driver when he would drive out for a good many years when he was called out.

The barber said, "You switched horses."

Henry said, "No. I asked you if you was sure you wanted *him*." He wanted the barber to go with us because he wouldn't think we switched horses on him.

Old Man Ganter's Hospitality

Croughan, whose tender-hearted side was exposed a few pages back, could also be tough and mean when he had to be, and roaders had frequent occasions, traveling as they were in the other man's territory, to show a little muscle when backing up a bargain that left a local boy with the short end of things. Croughan was a big man, according to the reports, and he also had a keen mind, and he knew both horses and men. He could suit his mien to fit the situation with the skill of an international diplomat.

Croughan showed his burly side in a story he told about a surly farmer he encountered on one of the many trading trips he made. This material was collected from Croughan on 14 April 1941, by Harold J. Moss.

He was a dark-visaged, overbearing sort and he just stood and watched me through his yard. In the west a rapidly rising dark bank of clouds was blotting out the late afternoon sun and there was an occasional rumble of thunder in the distance. The place looked prosperous enough but there was no welcome in the attitude of its burly, coarse-featured proprietor. Still, the coming storm forced me to call a halt for the day and set up camp in shape to weather one of those central Nebraska summer wind and rain storms.

I had no intention of asking this man for permission to camp in his yard. All I wanted was to get a few pails of water for my string of horses. "Howdy, neighbor," I hailed him. "What's the chances of getting some water for my horses. They're pretty dry."

He just stood there and eyed me for an interval, not even bothering to return my greeting. It was a little awkward, but I'd experienced something of the kind before, so I swung down from the board of my canvas-covered wagon and unhooked two big watering pails from the undergear.

He scowled as I did that and broke the silence, though his tone of voice was insolent enough: "Stranger, I don't calculate to let every Tom, Dick, and Harry outfit off the road water their diseased stock out of my tank." He spat out a thick stream of tobacco juice as if to emphasize his insulting remark.

"Well, neighbor," I said as curtly and evenly as I could under the circumstances, "I've got pails and there's no danger that way. Besides, it's going to storm and right soon now I'll have to get fixed for it." With that I started toward his stock tank with my pails.

He started toward me but evidently changed his mind and, wheeling around, he marched off toward the house. I watched him out of the tail of my eye as he entered the kitchen screened-in porch. A fellow like that might do most anything and I half expected to see him come out with a shotgun. But he didn't, and I went ahead with my watering. A middle-aged woman and a nice-looking girl about eighteen years old were busying themselves, setting table on that porch, evidently getting the evening meal ready.

The storm was closing in. In fact, the thunder was growing louder and more protracted. Though it was still early for a

73

summer evening the chickens were hurrying to roost as it grew darker and darker. By the time I finished watering the horses the farmer and his family, including two men who looked like hired hands, had seated themselves at the long table on the porch and were pitching into the victuals spread out along the table.

They worked fast.

The green-yellowish clouds boiled high overhead, above an inky black bank which reached to the horizon, unbroken by any light spots or openings. It was a thick storm and the signs were all for hail, wind and torrents of rain. I hurried over to the porch to thank that unfriendly farmer for his water and to also ask him where I could make a hurry-up camp. He looked sullenly into his half emptied plate, only lifting his eyes once, to shoot a dirty look at me as I approached. The two men acted indifferent but the woman and his two daughters—as I took them to be—appeared more friendly.

"Neighbor," I said standing outside and talking through the screen, "I want to thank you for the water and ask you if you can direct me to a handy place where I can get things ship-shape in a hurry before this storm hits."

A sharp crack of thunder exploded overhead and rolled away into the distance. The air hummed and vibrated. He just kept stuffing his gullet and looking down into the plate like a spoiled kid. One of the girls spoke up and said, "Dad, it's going to storm. Why don't you ask the gentleman to stay here until it's over? He can put his horses out in that old cow shed."

"Just keep your oar out of this," he half snarled at her.

I never saw a more ungracious human being. Then he addressed me, though he still looked down into his plate: "Stranger, I'm keepin' a farm here, not a hotel and livery stable. The best place for you to go and camp is to hit down that road out there and go a mile and a half in either direction away from here."

"Thanks again for the water," I told him, "and to hell with you for the rest of your stinking devilishness!" And with that I went to the wagon and turning around in his yard I drove out to the road and down along it about twenty rods to a wide,

74

level, grassy plot. There was another farm house just a few rods away on the other side. As I unhitched the wagon team and hobbled out the rest of my trading stock the lightening popped and crackled while the thunder crashed now instead of grumbling. I could see the lighter gray rain hang under the blue-black cloud mass, lifting itself in the west. That meant a downpour. The horses were nervous and uneasy but I did the best I could to make them comfortable, only I had to hobble most of them. I had one though—a highstrung little mare— that I felt a little uneasy about. She didn't like the storm.

Just as I was preparing to get into the wagon and start a little supper I heard a shout from the direction of that farm house on the other side of the road. A tall, spare fellow was hurrying toward my outfit motioning excitedly. As he came closer he pointed toward the tumbling clouds and ragged rain line a few miles to the west.

"Hurry, friend," he panted, "and come to my house. This is going to be a bad one." It looked it too, and I was worried. I yelled to him and told him about the mare. "Bring her along to the barn," he said. "But hurry up. That thing's about to bust!"

We got the mare up to his place, just as the first sheet of rain came sweeping in from the west. We put her in the barn and when I looked out again you couldn't see to the road. The wind smashed against the barn and it shivered and shook. Then, just as I had feared, the hail started with a sharp report like cracks against the boards of the roof and side.

The friendly farmer asked me to stay to supper and I told him I sure would—but that right then I worried about my horses. As yet the hail wasn't so thick but the stones were big enough to scare the horses. There wasn't much I could do but I decided to make it back to the wagon. I couldn't see it to the horses through that gray wall of rain. My friend cussed me for a darned fool but I went out and splashed through six inches of rushing water in the lane and waded up the road, which was already partly flooded.

Three or four hailstones hit me and one knocked me half dizzy. The horses were huddled around the wagon—all but one, a ten-dollar buckskin mare with the asthma heaves. I never hobbled her and she had made off. After the storm I could find out her whereabouts; there wasn't much I could do now, only crawl into the wagon and keep an eye on my hobbled horses while I changed my soaked clothes for dry ones.

That was a ripper of a storm and the whole countryside was a lake. Lightning flared and swooped continuously, and purple balls of fire seemed to just float through the air. For two hours it poured, though the hail soon let up. There must have been five inches of rain.

When the main storm had passed and the rain was tailing off into a drizzle the tall, lanky farmer came sloshing up through the water and mud and, after looking over my outfit, he told me to come to his house for supper. I was glad to do it too, for my wagon was pretty wet inside. I mentioned the buckskin mare that had wandered away but didn't go into details, such as to how little I cared whether she ever showed up again.

Up to now our interest being centered on the storm I hadn't told him about the little experience with his neighbor up the road. On the way to his house I told him about it. "Yeah," he said, "I saw you in there and you must have had him kinda overpowered. He usually chases travelers right out. He's a big bluff though and he won't hardly sleep a wink tonight worryin' about you bein' camped out so near to him. You know, he always frets and stews about somebody's slippin' in and robbin' him or knockin' them on the heads or something. His name is Ganter. Mine's Lindley."

I told him my name was Croughan and we got along fine.

After supper and just at dusk he suggested that he run over to Ganter's and see if my buckskin had strayed in there. I went with him as far as the wagon and after seeing that the horses were all right and there and in good order, I set about making my wagon fit for the night. Lindley came by after a bit and he told me that the buckskin mare was there and that Ganter had put her in the cowshed. He, so Lindley said, was worried about a stranger like me being in the neighborhood and would have liked it better if I had moved on.

76

Early the next morning, about six o'clock, I was up and around, looking after the horses, when Ganter's wife and one of his daughters came down the road toward me. Mrs. Ganter was very apologetic in her bearing but she didn't mention that husband of hers. Instead she asked me if I wouldn't come up to breakfast—seeing that I had put through a hard night after the big storm. She didn't let on that they knew I had been over to Lindley's for supper. The girl joined in with her mother in inviting me but I told them I couldn't make it. They even offered to bring me something down to the wagon.

All at once the Ganter family was getting friendly. I just decided to stay around there a couple of days. It might bother old Ganter and I might turn a few good trades.

That afternoon Lindley came over to the wagon and wanted to know if I cared to trade the little mare. (He didn't know she kicked.) "There's a fellow over to my place right now that's interested and he ought to be easy. He's a bootlegger and has some cash."

"Has he got some heavy moonshine along?" I asked him. "If he has, I'll be right over."

"Well," Lindley remarked, "he just drove in and if he hasn't it's the first time he ever came along without a few jugs!"

He had me interested now and I went along back with him to meet "Bootlegger" Dan Monishee. Dan was a bright-eyed, medium-sized individual who appeared to be looking in all directions at once. Still, he seemed perfectly relaxed and at ease, though a bit cautious. Of all the rigs for a bootlegger to be driving around the country, he had a big, brown, slow mule hitched up to an old surrey! We got acquainted right off and he asked me how I liked Farmer Ganter over the way. I guess Lindley had mentioned something about the way he had treated me. I told him with a few short cuss words.

It turned out that he was in the market for a single driver and he was willing to deal that brown mule. Then he winked and added, "You can have choice of color, brown or white." I could see that we were going to get along great now that I knew he had his "white mule" [extra good moonshine, with devastating kick] along with him. We traded all right: he gave me that big, slow mule, thirty dollars in cash, and a gallon of moonshine whiskey for my little mare. I told him that the little mare occasionally got a little nervous and so forgot herself as to kick now and then. That didn't seem to bother him any, so I guessed he either was used to kicking horses or else had no experience at all with them.

Just in case she might go on a kicking rampage and hurt my bootlegger friend—maybe break up a few jugs of his moonshine—I helped him put a kicking strap on her. She behaved real decent when he hitched her up. Before he drove away, he pulled out a pint bottle of what he called his "Grade A Private Stock" and the three of us celebrated the trade in regular style. It must have been about 150 proof, for it had a kick like a real mule. Dan posed as a stock and grain buyer, just as a front, he said, and actually did quite a lot of business in that line. Somehow I had the idea that he gave away as much moonshine as he sold but still it was good salesmanship. I watched him drive down the road and the mare, busy picking her way through the mud, never made any effort to kick. If she had, she would have set down on her hind end with that kicking strap tied in. She really was a slick little piece of horse flesh except for her occasional kicking spell.

The trade was sure satisfactory to me all the way 'round and that mule was sound and of good size. I'm not so sure about the "white" variety but it came in handy when I "talked turkey" to that buzzard of a Ganter later on.

That was the best part of the whole business, and he asked for it himself. I wouldn't ever have given him the satisfaction of having me come to him. It happened this way.

He got to looking at that ten-dollar heavy buckskin mare while she was still in his cowshed after the storm, but he evidently didn't look very close. I sent Lindley up to get her and pay him for her keep if any, and Ganter put out a feeler as to the chances of a trade. When Lindley brought the mare back, he told me about it and added that Ganter must have some scheme in mind to give me the short end of the stick, as he was never known to try a deal where he couldn't get the best of it. He didn't even charge anything for the mare's keep, and Lindley said that that in itself was enough to make anyone suspicious who knew Ganter's notorious reputation for charging three prices for everything, if he could get it.

The next morning Ganter came out and fooled around, pretending to fix his fence along the road. He was, it was plain to see, just using that as an excuse to get down to my outfit without appearing to do so. He moved along, testing the strands of wire—even drove a few staples, and finally got within talking distance.

"Good morning, Mr. Croughan," he greeted me in what was to him a pleasant voice. He had learned my name probably from Lindley and was damned polite all of a sudden, considering his cussedness the day of the storm.

I just grunted and went about my chores. He came on to the wagon, then stood around sort of sheepish and gawked at the horses. I said nothing. It looked pretty much like he had a purpose in coming. He did too.

"Mr. Croughan, I got to looking at your mare when she was up there in my shed and you know, I need a horse about that size to match in. I can give you a good trade because I've got a big six-year-old that you can turn at a good profit. I could do it myself but I'm too busy."

He gave me that line and I wondered what was wrong with his big six-year-old. There must sure have been something. Just to string the old duck along a little, I said, "No, Mr. Ganter, I don't care to have any truck with you after the way you treated me."

"Oh that!" he said a little nervously. "I wasn't feeling very good that day. A storm always upsets me."

He sure had swallowed his pride all right. He was a persistent cuss though. I'll say that for him. I told him I didn't feel like stepping foot on his precious place, but instead of being insulted he eagerly offered to bring his horse down to my camp and before I could put up any objection he was off hot-footin' up to his place to get that horse.

Directly he was back, leading a big, rangy bay that looked smooth and well-gaited, a good mover, and darned if he looked a day over six-years old, just as Ganter had said. The only thing I could think of was concealed defects, or else Ganter expected to extract big cash boot out of me.

While he was after his horse I took a good shot out of that jug of Dan's moonshine and by the time the old boy returned I was in splendid form to handle him, no matter what the hitch in the deal might be. Why in hell he wanted that buckskin mare was beyond me unless he was just a chump as far as horses were concerned. He told me his bay was well broke and worked every day. Said he had been on the plow all spring. That remark gave me something to think about, for that horse's shoulders were clean as a hound's tooth, not a callous mark on them.

Now, plow work is pretty stiff and usually scuffs a horse's shoulders. It began to look very much like Ganter was trying to hand me a "cold-shouldered" horse—in other words, a balky one. And, I thought, if that's the case he must be a bad case or "my friend" Ganter wouldn't be so anxious to trade him off. But I didn't say anything about it for the time, thinking maybe that by leading him on I could have a little fun.

So I fooled around for a while and listened to Ganter tell what a hell of a good horse he had. Finally I run my hands up and down that bay's shoulders and made a few remarks about how smooth his shoulders were for a plow horse. Ganter said something about having new collars that fit as easy as feather pillows.

Now a balky horse will drive some people nearly distracted, but they never bothered me much. With a little patience and the right kind of gear you can usually bring them out of the habit.

"Well, how do you want to trade?" I asked him.

"Even," he replied, "though I ought to have fifty dollars to boot."

Of course he couldn't have known that the buckskin was heavey as hell: the weather wasn't hot and sultry enough. I didn't expect he'd offer even up and wondered if the big bay had something else wrong with him. I decided to ask ten dollars cash boot myself since he didn't ask any. That buckskin had never done two hours steady work that I ever knew about, but I had her harness-marked all right. You do that by rubbing a little croton oil on the hair and it leaves scars that look just like harness marks.

Ganter kicked up some at the mention of cash boot and I couldn't blame him, but his protest was anything but determined, and damned if he didn't offer me five dollars boot. He didn't even ask me if the buckskin was sound, but I told him that she wouldn't do so good if she got over-heated! "Neither would any horse," he said a little spiritedly, "but I never over-heat my horses."

I made no further comment and we traded "as is" though I doubt if he even knew what went in a horse trade.

The buckskin was a little "snorty" as he led her up the road and I wondered whether he intended to work her that day. I intended to stay till the next day, and I didn't give a rap how soon he found out about her heaves, as he was sure to do once he put her in the collar. She couldn't work fifteen minutes without blowing up.

That night Lindley came over for a visit and incidentally to take a few pulls at my jug. He was speechless with surprise when I told him about the trade. "Ganter must be slipping," he said, as much to himself as to me, "or else he feels stinkin' about the way he treated you. Though that would be a miracle. I'll bet a ten-dollar dog he'll be around all right when he finds out how worthless the buckskin is—if you're still here."

"I think I'll be here," I told him. He was sure to find out whenever he tried to work the old snide and I was a little curious to hear what he'd have to say.

He must have tried out his new horse that next morning, for about 11 o'clock he came striding down the middle of the road toward my outfit, and he wasn't loafing along either. "What in hell's wrong with that horse you traded me?" he roared.

"Why," I said, "plenty, I'd guess from the way you're rearin' up on your hind legs." His face was red as a beet and he looked like he was about to go into a fit.

He let go another blast then: "I told those damned-fool women of mine that you was just a road bum, and they had the

81

gall to say that you seemed such a nice, pleasant man. Well, what you goin' to do about that worthless plug you put off onto me?"

"Not a damned thing," I told him. "You had it comin' to you anyway for the scurvy way you treated me the other day, and you remember that you asked for it yourself. I told you I didn't want any truck with you."

"I'll knock your head off. I'll have the law on you!" he howled.

I took a couple of steps toward him and he backed away. "You can try either one if you want to," I told him. "You're a hell of a horse trader and an all around mean skunk. It would be a pleasure to wrap this neck yoke around your lousy neck." I made a grab for it, though I didn't have the least idea of hitting him.

But he thought I meant business and he turned tail and ran up the road toward his house. That night two of his girls slipped down to the wagon and said, "Pa wasn't feelin' well but he would trade back even and let you keep the five dollars."

I told them to tell him nothing doing.

That's the last I heard from him, though the next morning just as I was pulling out I saw him lead the buckskin out and turn her into a small pasture. She stopped dead in the gate and he gave her a whack on the rump. She must have been in the middle of one of her bad spells. She tottered on out into the pasture a little ways and stood there with her head drooping down between her legs. He must have given her a hell of a workout, though I had the idea that he wanted a light horse for driving and light work. Any way you looked at it, she wouldn't have been any good—heavy work, light work, or no work at all. He had it coming to him.

The big bay he traded to me was balky—cold-shouldered—just as I thought, but outside of that he was sound as an agate stone. I hitched him in with one of my best pullers, put on a hackmore—that's a hitch from his nose to the double tree—and after he hung back a few times and that hitch tightened on his breathing, he quit his hanging back and kept moving.

He was a good looker and of course I aimed to deal him to good advantage. Ganter must have been a poor hand with horses to let a balky horse get the best of him and then make the sap trade he did. I put a few harness marks on him with croton oil and sometime later I traded him to a farmer for a smooth-mouthed middle-weight dapple gray, a set of harness—and twenty-seven dollars and fifty cents cash boot. Maybe Ganter didn't know it, but he paid pretty dear for his meanness the day of the storm.

Part II: *HORSES*

Lou and Dexter Find the Gate

*Horses have their share of flamboyant and even spectacular
physical ailments and defects, as you will see, but in my opinion
the stories that tell us the most about horses are those that
portray some quirk or curiosity of equine psychology, like the
tales of this group.*

*This tale was collected from Lew Croughan by Harold J.
Moss on 12 November 1940.*

A horse is a smart animal and when they travel in a trading
outfit they develop their technique to a high degree. Once I
had a blind mare by the name of Lou and a twelve-hundred
pound horse called Dexter. Lou was a dapple brown mare and
Dexter was a chestnut sorrel, being also my best wagon horse.
He knew all the answers, including the one about the farmer's
corn fields along the way.

Along just before camp time Dexter always began to
inspect the fields and fences on either side of the road. He was
looking for convenient openings in the field. The horse just
naturally exerted himself to be helpful in the business of
acquiring a little free grain. Dexter knew that camp was going
to be made fairly close to a good corn field—that is, in season—
and he had the openings spotted, if there were any.

When we stopped and made ready for camp I always
hobbled the horses and let them forage along the road. The
blind mare, Lou, always stuck close to Dexter and he led her
around, keeping an eye on her to see that she didn't get into
any ditches or holes.

Well, I hobbled the horses with torn gunny sacks, knotting
the sacks and tying the front legs together below the knees,
leaving just enough play so that they could graze along by
moving each front foot a few inches at a time. But Dexter had

learned that he could do better and go farther by hopping along like a rabbit, and the blind mare learned to follow him in a like fashion

On this particular evening we camped (as you might guess) by a very substantial corn field, which was then pretty well matured. It looked to be pretty tight fenced and, off hand, I thought Dexter for once was stumped as far as getting into the corn field was concerned. I was mistaken, for a little after dark I missed Dexter and the blind mare. They had wandered away somewhere and I couldn't even hear any sound of them about. The other horses were hobbling around eating grass and I didn't worry any about those two. Dexter always played that trick the same way; he'd slip away, sometimes alone, in the dark but he would always be back before daylight. And sure enough, the next morning in the first gray light of dawn, when I turned out, there he was, and Lou, the blind mare, with him standing docilely a few feet away from the wagon.

Before we got ready to pull out, I decided to go back along the road, just out of curiosity, and see if he had spotted an opening into the field, for I couldn't recall seeing one the evening before. He and the mare seemed well fed up on something.

And sure enough, back about a quarter of a mile, at a cross fence line, was an open gate. Dexter had remembered it and led that blind mare up there and into the field, where they had filled up on corn. Dexter had been with me a long time, and an old trading outfit horse gets into the corn field dodge just like his owner.

An itinerant trader's horses, if they spend enough time on the road, always get a thrill out of a covered wagon. Many a time I have been driving past a farmer's pasture and an old snide would throw his head up when he saw my outfit, whinny, and start over to us. They get to like the road and a covered wagon means as much to them as a fire truck does to a fire horse.

88

I Just Give Her a Good Whalin'
with a Stay Chain

*Andrew Dickson, another horse trader who was interviewed
extensively by WPA workers in 1939 and 1940, was in many
ways the antithesis of Lew Croughan. He operated in Otoe
County, Nebraska, in the 1880s and 1890s like Croughan, but
he was quiet and slight and his guile was more subtle than
Croughan's. He had "keen perception and knowledge of
equines," according to the fieldworker's reports, and he had a
"mysterious manner." Dickson's trade was primarily in those
circles that restricted the degree of investigation and examination that the traders could employ: "Horse traders depend on
their own wits and in a flat-footed trade, a good trader never
asks to run a horse around or give him a workout. That is a
sort of gentleman's agreement, an unwritten code, but thoroughly understood, and if one is outsmarted by the other, no
quarter is asked."*

*Andrew Dickson's nephew was also named Dickson, and
he too dabbled to some extent in horse trades, though his main
business was farming. Mr. Dickson recalled a story of a horse
trade in which his nephew became involved.*

One day a local resident of the community, who went by the
nickname of "Dinger," came along and stopped to talk horses
with the boys. My nephew was somewhat in the notion of
getting a different horse for field work and he sounded "Dinger" out on the subject.

"Yes," said "Dinger," "I've got a good worker if she's handled right. Outside of bein' an ornery color, you ought to get
along with her."

Well, they got together on a trade and "Dinger" talked my
nephew out of fifteen dollars boot and a moon-eyed ten-year-
old plug for that mouse-colored mare. She had a familiar look
somehow, but none of us could say offhand just why.

As my nephew tells it, for several days that mare worked
right along, right up in the collar and handlin' nice on the plow

89

on a four-horse hitch. Then I had some hay to haul and hitched her up with one of my best pullers since we had some soft ground in the meadow. I noticed that she, when hitched to the hayrack, had taken to twisting her head around and looking back at me, as if she was trying to figure out something. I began to do a little figuring myself, for that's the way a balky horse will often do, mostly to see if you've got a whip handy.

The second day, as we were starting to the barn with a good jag of hay, she did that again and that time she stopped dead in her tracks and refused to move. She wouldn't go another step, even after I belted her good with a knotted rope.

A balky horse was something I never did want around, so I sent the hired man to get another horse and then we took her out of the harness. I told him to go ahead with the hay and I set right out to trade that mare off.

About five miles south of our place I traded her to a farmer by the name of Hendricks for a raw-boned gray that looked to be about fourteen years old. Hendricks and I traded as is and no guarantee, expressed or implied. Afterward he told me what happened. He put her on a four-horse hitch, using a set of old Concord harness, with chain tugs. She just dug right in and didn't even look back like she got to doing with me.

After a few days he fitted her out with a leather harness with leather tugs and went to working her double. This went all right for a day or so and then she started looking back at him and suddenly stopped dead and balked. He tried all the tricks he knew but she wouldn't budge. Mad clear through Hendricks took her out of the harness and led her to the barn. It might have just been a happenstance, but "Dinger," the fellow who traded her to me in the first place, came along at about that time and stopped in at Hendrick's. He eyed that mouse-colored mare in a speculative manner but said nothing about having seen her before. Instead, he seemed only bent on a neighborly call. But neighborly call or not, before he left he traded that same old plug I traded to him for the balky mare and got fifteen dollars more to boot out of Hendricks and besides he had the original mare back as well as my fifteen dollars.

90

Hendricks probably would have stopped to consider if he had given a little time to the matter, but he was mad clear through with that balky mare.

"Dinger," who was not ordinarily given to discussing his trading transactions with others, let drop a few remarks and the story got around. That mare was a distinct asset to him. He had come into possession of her quite a bit previous to all this and having worked her some found out that she balked after a few days of good behavior, just as Hendricks and I had experienced. But "Dinger," being a little curious, went to the farmer he got her from and, after a little sparring around, he found out more about her.

"Yes," the farmer said, "she used to balk a 'leetle' but I 'lowed she was plum all over that, else I'd told you about it." Of course "Dinger" knew better than that, knowing horse trading as he did.

"Well, how'd you keep her from it," "Dinger" wanted to know.

"I just give her a good whalin' with a stay chain," the farmer told him. "Plain whippin' and other persuadin' didn't do no good, but when I whaled her with that stay chain she jumped right out of her balk. All I had to do after that was carry that piece of chain along and rattle it on the wagon box once in a while when she started gittin' fancy notions."

"Dinger" began to see why the mare didn't balk with Hendricks as long as he used the Corncord harness with the chain tugs. He tried out the chain business and sure enough it worked and since the mare was really a good, sound, all-around horse, otherwise, he soon began to get ideas about using her as a stock trader, which he could deal off at a good profit and get back for a song each time. It was for that reason that he didn't bother to tell any of his victims the simple remedy in case she balked. He just kept track of who had her and managed to be on hand at the right moment. Anyway, a horse trader who would have been so honest as to tell a prospect that his own horse was balky would soon be classed as being a trifle touched in the head.

Cocaine for the Dummy

*The following tale, although not remarkable in narrative style
or content, offers an invaluable insight into the development
and training of the itinerant horse trader. It is clear that a good
deal of the professional trader's education came from the School
of Hard Knocks and that before the swapper was able to operate
profitably in the field he had to endure his share of losses at the
hands of the professors at that venerable school. The material is
obviously from Lew Croughan, and while we lack full documentation, it seems likely that it was collected by Harold J. Moss in
late 1940 or early 1941.*

I returned to eastern Nebraska in the 90's, where a fellow
named Abe Sissler taught me the horse-trading business. It
cost me plenty for the lessons. He skinned me out of four
hundred dollars before I began to see how it was done. Sissler,
after taking all my money, let me stay with him the rest of the
winter free, and even outfitted me in the spring with a few old
plugs to use as trading stock.

I started out, camping along the road, and managed to hit
on some good trades in the northeastern part of the state. I
was learning fast too, and discovering some new wrinkles
which most traders didn't know. You see, a professional horse
trader is always on the lookout for stock he can trade on. These
would be horses that looked good but had hidden defects which
could be temporarily fixed up. If the hidden defect was bad
enough, a good trader could always count on getting back the
horse for a song.

I soon found that the average farmer is a poor horse trader.
Consequently I began thinking I could shut my eyes and give
all of them a good skinning. But I was soon fooled when, in
Burt County, I ran across an innocent looking farmer who,
somehow, impressed me as being a most religious sort. He had
a kindly smile and that apologetic manner which most easy
marks seem to be endowed with. His name was Hubbard.

"Stranger," says he, "I always stayed shy of hoss tradin'. Seems how I just don't like to think maybe I'd be cheating somebody." Here he quoted something about, "Treat your brother as you would yourself."

The old rascal, after his quotation, hesitated a little and peered at me—I guess to see how I was reacting to his talk on how much he enjoyed being honest. He had thrown me clear off my guard with his remark, until I thought, "Here is a sucker, if I can get him into a trade."

That wasn't as hard as I thought it would be, although I was a little surprised when he agreed to talk trade provided I would agree not to let him skin me. Here was something new in horse trading, for me anyway, but I immediately agreed to his proposition and told him to show me his stock. Still acting hesitant and apologetic he went into the barn to reappear shortly leading a spirited looking black six-year-old, which really looked as smooth and sound as anything I'd seen for a long time. That horse had lots of action too and he was well gaited and stepped around as lively as anyone could want. In fact he looked so good I couldn't help wondering why Hubbard wanted to trade him.

He agreed to consider one of my string, a pretty little brown mare, who was about as sound as any horse I have ever had for trading purposes. The farmer kept on hemming and hawing and talking about not wanting to trick anybody, but his conscience didn't bother him enough to prevent him from asking twenty-five dollars cash boot.

His black was a better horse—or so I thought—and it looked to me as if he had twenty-five dollars difference in his favor. He had me going good, so I shucked out twenty-five dollars cash boot, threw in a halter with my brown mare, and drove off leading his black horse. Hubbard watched me as I drove off without seeming much interested in his new brown mare.

Along toward evening I began looking around for a suitable camp. Suitable camp spots for a horse trader are apt to be handy to some farmer's cornfield. I finally found a good location and pulled up to a stop.

93

Then things began to happen. I had my new black hitched to the back of the middle section of the wagon with four other horses spread out to its sides. The wagon and horses stopped except the black horse, who kept coming until he had smacked into the back end. Then, instead of stopping, he continued pushing the wagon. At first I thought he was blind, but a blind horse would have stopped when he felt the wagon. This horse continued pushing so hard that I had difficulty in getting the outfit stopped. When I finally got around to the back end of the wagon, the black was leaning against the wheels. His eyes had a glazed appearance. What had happened to the horse was beyond me. I couldn't figure him out.

I decided to drive on further and see what would happen. This time after the slack was taken out of the black's halter rope there was a jerk that shook the wagon. I looked back and saw the horse, looking kind of dazed, being literally dragged along. He was just letting himself go, not holding back and still not walking. Thinking he was sick I decided to make camp where I was and let him rest up.

He wouldn't eat or drink and just stood where he was, still behind the wagon. He stayed right there all night without moving out of his tracks.

The next morning I couldn't get the black to eat until I thought of the trick of rubbing oats in his mouth. Once he started eating he couldn't stop. As an experiment I poured half a bushel of oats into a basket. I felt certain he couldn't eat many of them. But before I got around to see how he was doing he had emptied the basket and was looking around for more.

We finally got under way, although I nearly pulled the black off his feet before he got going. He sure was acting funny, and I was rapidly realizing there was more the matter with him than I had thought. After traveling about two miles down the road I spotted a likely looking farm place with some good looking horses in a pasture. A dark-whiskered man was coming out of the place into the road. I took him to be the farmer, but he turned out to be a local horse doctor who had just completed a professional call.

94

He was driving a long, rangy sorrel, hitched to a two-wheel cart. Now a good horse trader never passes by any prospect, so I hailed him. He pulled up and waited until my outfit was even with him. Forgetting about the queer behaviour of my new black horse I stopped my team—or tried to. But the black just walked on into the back of the wagon and started pushing it ahead. The whiskered man stared at the odd performance. The black finally got himself stopped, then stood leaning against the wagon, motionless as a statue.

The fellow didn't say anything for the time and I felt uneasy, hardly knowing how to proceed. However, he broke the ice himself by asking, "What's ailin' your horse, Mister?"

This was a poser for me, for I sure didn't know, but I thought up an answer which turned out to be a pretty lame one. "Why, stranger," I replied, "that horse has been worked as a pusher on heavy hauling and he just naturally thinks the lead team needs a little more help."

He studied the black for a while and looked skeptical, then he untangled his long frame from the dinky cart and dismounted to examine the black at close range. He jockeyed the other horses to the side, untied the black, and tried to lead him around. But the horse just stood where he was, looking more than ever as if he had been carved out of stone.

"Humph! Just as I thought. You got a dummy there, young feller. Not many of them around these parts. Fact is, I don't ever recollect seein' one myself, but I know about them, all right. I'm an old horseman and horse doctor. Where'd you get him?"

I had to do a little quick thinking before replying, but decided that the truth would serve for once, so I told him about the apologetic Mr. Hubbard who was so anxious not to skin anybody.

"Yeh, I know that old buzzard, all right, but where he could have gotten that dummy is beyond me. I know he didn't have it around the last time I was up that way."

For once the wind was taken clean out of my sails, as a horse trader, and I just looked dumb, not even knowing how to approach the situation.

"Will he eat or drink, and if he does, will he stop once he gets started?" my new friend continued.

"Well," I replied, "I did have some trouble getting him to eat and drink, but he had to stop when there was no more feed or water."

"Well, sonny,"—he never addressed me in the same way twice—"I'm going to tell you something about dummy horses. There ain't many of them but you can have a pile of fun with them if you know how, specially when you're in the trading business."

"A dummy," he went on, "is nearly always a likely looking hoss, better'n average for some reason, only they have a brain affliction which causes them to act the funny way they do. When they stop, they won't start, and when they start, they won't stop. That applies to about anything a horse is apt to do. A dummy, once he gets started, will drink water till he runs over, or eats grass till he is so packed full he *has* to quit. It's funny, but that's the way it works.

"But a trader, if he knows how to fix one, has a cinch takin' in suckers and gettin' his dummy back with a good profit each time. It's trading back-handed, all right, but any good trader knows that's one of the best tricks. So you should be able to trade your horse off for a fair animal and cash boot each time and get 'im back for a song, except when you tangle with someone who knows about dummies, and there ain't many of that stripe around.

"Here's how you fix 'em up, and it's simple enough. Just go to any drugstore and buy yourself some cocaine." [Cocaine could be bought by anyone in those days.] "Rub a little on the tonsils of the horse's tongue. He'll come right into life and look and act like a hundred-dollar animal."

Here my bewhiskered friend paused and regarded me quizzically. You could have knocked me over with a feather, it sounded so fantastic.

Then and there I discarded any idea I had had of approaching the stranger on a trade. Besides, I was anxious to try out the scheme and see if it worked as he had said it would. After

96

a few minutes of neighborly chatting we continued on our different ways and that was the last I saw of the horse doctor.

Finally I got some cocaine at the first drugstore I came to and lost no time in giving the black horse a dose according to the horse doctor's directions. Sure enough, the effect was almost instantaneous, and, to me, magical. The horse seemed to grow in size and began vibrating with life. He immediately reached for grass and started eating. He would start and stop like a normal horse, and appeared smoother than most horses. This amazing change fascinated me. It seemed almost unbelievable after the way I had been dragging him along and feeding him with a spoon, so to speak.

The idea of back-handed trading, as my advisor had expressed it, interested me. In theory, at least, I should be able to trade off the black on easy trades and get him back for practically nothing—that is, if the horse was kept in condtion.

That black attracted lots of attention along the road after the treatments and several proposed to deal for him. But I had other plans. I was thinking about foxy Abe Sissler and about his wife, who played three-card monte. With her card games she skinned me out of some of the four hundred dollars I mentioned at the beginning of the story. I felt certain I could get back from Abe some of the money he had taken from me if I kept the dummy fixed. So I changed my route and headed for Abe's part of the country, trading as I went, but turning down deals for the black.

In the course of a week I reached Abe Sissler's place, where I was received with open arms and practically ordered to make their place my headquarters. Abe spent some time in looking over my stock with particular attention to my black horse, who, with his charge of cocaine, was stepping high, wide, and handsome.

I didn't say much but waited for Abe to offer a trade. Sure enough, on the next day, he said, "Son, you wanta deal me that black for my sorrel mare Suzie? She's better'n your black, but I can match the black. What say we swap?"

Now, I didn't know much about his sorrel Suzie, and I didn't care either, for I figured I could blast some cash boot out of him and then get the black back at my own figure when the treatments were stopped and the black started to "dummy" again. So I held off until the next day, when I told Abe I was calculating to get going pretty quick.

"Hell," he says, "you ain't figuring to run away from that trade for the sorrel Suzie? That's a deal for you, with the twenty-five dollar boot I offered you." He hadn't made me any cash boot offer but I let it go at that and let him ease me into the deal.

Just to be dead sure the black wouldn't relapse into his dummy state too quickly I had given him an extra dose of cocaine that morning. It would have been awkward if he had relapsed too quickly. But that didn't happen and we made the deal, Abe handing over sorrel Suzie and twenty-five dollars, which was only a small part of the four hundred dollars he had taken away from me in the first place. I lost no time making a get-away for a couple of days, taking my whole string of horses, including the new sorrel mare.

But I planned to show up again when I was sure the black horse would have slid back into those dummy ways. In two days I went back and drove into Sissler's yard, as bold as brass. He heard me coming and appeared in the door of his barn with his sleeves rolled up and a dripping drench bottle in his hands.

"What? You back?" he shouted. "You're just in time. Got a sick horse here. It's the black you traded me. Maybe you know what ails him."

"Well now, that's funny. That horse was in good shape when I left," I said. But I went with Sissler to the barn, where the black was wedged up against the manger, which he had tried to walk through. His eyes were glassy and to one who didn't know, he looked like a horse who had died standing up.

"Don't that beat hell," roared Abe. "Never seen a horse act like that."

I naturally pretended to be utterly mystified, and went through a little hocus-pocus of examining the black. I had an idea for a little fun with Abe, so I asked, "Ever have a wind-locked horse?" I had never heard of one myself, but it sounded impressive.

98

"No," Abe answered. "Guess you mean wind colic."

"Well, no," I told him, "not exactly. It's different. The only chance of cure is a good soaping." Of course that was the same as an enema.

Abe, foxy as he was, began to prepare for the chore, although even the thought of it was distasteful to him. At the same time I could see that he wasn't quite convinced, because his puzzled expression indicated he suspected something was a little off-color.

But he went ahead with the messy operation, as I had suggested. While he was busy with the black I slipped around by the manger and gave the horse a small dose of cocaine. I timed this just about right, giving him the cocain at the same time Sissler was through with his work. The horse, true to his Dr. Jekyll and Mr. Hyde personality, immediately stepped smartly around the stall and reached for hay. When he saw the transformation, Abe rubbed his eyes in surprise. Of course he thought that the water and soap had done the trick. But still he looked a little juggerous.

"Danged if it didn't work! But hell, I never seen a critter get cured that fast before, and seein's there wasn't much 'action,' I reckon it's something new in hoss ailments."

"I wouldn't wonder if it was myself," I told him, trying hard to keep from laughing in his face. I hadn't given the black a very big dose, so it began to wear off towards nightfall. It's funny, but the horse took more time to get back to dummying than he did coming out of it.

Abe kept an eye on him and saw that the horse was getting a little queer again, like he was before. He decided on another soaping and while he was about it I gave the black another small dose of cocaine. The same thing happened again, with the horse recovering so quickly it looked as if a miracle had taken place. Abe looked thoughtful.

"Hell," he said, "if I have to keep a-doin' this danged business to keep that plug in condition, I think I'll get rid of him. This here business is a tarnation nuisance."

"Oh, he'll be all right tomorrow," I told him. "he's probably all right now." Which he was—but not for long.

The next morning, as I suspected, the black was back to his dummy ways and wouldn't eat or drink. Abe looked disgusted while I tried to keep a straight face. "Maybe he needs some feed, Abe," I told him.

"Well, now, I don't care much if he ever eats," Abe snorted. But just the same, he brought a measure of oats and threw them in the feed box. The horse just stood there and made no effort to eat. He didn't even move.

"Here. Let me see," I said, as I stepped up to the feed box. There I picked up a handful of oats and rubbed them on the black's muzzle. He trembled a little and muzzled my hand easy-like, then started to eat. Gently I lowered his head into the feed, where he began eating like a machine.

"I think all that horse needs is a good feeding," I told Abe.

Abe looked at me kind of squint-eyed and snorted, "By God, if that's what's ailing the danged fool, he'll get the feeding of his life." And with that remark Abe brought over a half-bushel measure of oats and dumped them in with the first ones.

Well, that dummy hung over the feed box and kept munching away. He was just about down to the bottom of the box when Abe returned from his other chores to take a look. "Hell's fire," he roared, "that's the all-firedest eatin' plug I ever seen."

"Give him some more oats, Abe. That's what he needs," I advised. I had an idea that the black would, true to his dummy disposition, eat all morning. And he would have too, if Abe hadn't given up in disgust.

"That's a hell of a horse you worked off on me," Abe muttered with a scowl on his broad, weather-beaten face. "First he won't eat, then won't stop eating. And that bushel of oats— enough for four horses—doesn't even begin to fill him up."

I had planned to tell Abe what really was the matter with the black but decided to wait, meantime calling on the farmers in the neighborhood with my string. When I returned the next day, Abe had somehow managed to get the black out of the barn. He had him over by the corncrib, which the horse was now trying to push over. Abe opened up with a string of cuss words a mile long when he saw me pull up into the yard.

"Hell's oats," he yelled, "your danged black plug almost walked over me. Now he is trying to push over the crib."

Abe didn't know about the black's habit of keeping right on once he was started. And I noticed that he referred to the black as "your danged black plug." Knowing that crafty old Abe knew some of the cocaine tricks I began to wonder if during my absence he had heard something about dummies. I decided then and there to find out.

"Abe," says I, "ever hear about a dummy horse?" The old boy looked blank, so I figured he hadn't. "Well," I continued, "I'm going to be brutally frank with you and tell you what you got there. That's a dummy horse."

"What in hell's a dummy horse?" he came back at me.

Then I told him what I had learned through experience about dummies, adding that I had in mind the four hundred dollars he had taken from me, or I wouldn't have played the horse off on him.

"Of course, of course. I know you wouldn't have done that, sonny, if I hadn't skinned you first." But he knew I would have.

I asked him why he was throwing good money after bad, but he just looked wise and told me not to worry about that. It was plain to see that Abe already had a plan, and was well satisfied.

Well sir, he started in on a long string of back-handed trades with that dummy, getting him back each time. He ranged over quite a territory, keeping the horse high-stepping with the cocaine treatment. Afterwards he told me one fellow he traded the dummy to was so disgusted he gave back the dummy just to be rid of him

But a funny thing happened. Abe ran into a easy looking old hayseed farmer on one of his jaunts who, Abe said, didn't even have the cockleburs combed out of his whiskers. The old boy took to the black dummy—Abe had him charged up—and offered to trade. Abe, cocksure that he would get the dummy back for little or nothing, traded even for a ragged-looking gray that was none too promising, but had plenty of action. As he drove home he reflected that he would like to see Old

Whiskers when he discovered the inevitable queer change in the black.

But Abe had a bigger surprise coming to him. Later he told me, "When I got the gray horse home that night he seemed tired, so I turned him out into a small yard that was closed in with a board fence. During the night I heard a racket but didn't get up. The next morning, when I went out, danged if I didn't find the gray had walked right through the fence and was trying to eat his way through a load of hay on the hay rack in the outside yard. It looked like given a little time, he would manage to do it too. He was pushing against the hay rack and eating hay for all he was worth. He had already downed half of the jag of hay when I found him.

"I had a thundering hard tussle to get him away from there. The only thing that stopped him was the barn. I couldn't help having an uneasy feeling that the old rube with the long whiskers had put something over on me. In fact, it looked as if he had swapped dummies with me and had gotten the best looking dummy out the of deal.

"And that's just what the old buzzard had done too. The black was a good looking piece of trading stock, while that gray—even if he hadn't been a dummy—was a no-account. Old Whiskers wouldn't trade back either. He knew how to handle dummies and the black was a heap-better looker. Where in the tarnation he could have gotten hold of that gray dummy is beyond me, for they're scarcer than hen's teeth."

Abe got tired of trying to deal that gray dummy. He finally traded him to a tin-horn trader for a two-dollar saddle. I never found out what happened to the black.

Look That Team Over Pretty Carefully

Back-trading was such a profitable business that when horses with hard-to-detect, easy-to-cover flaws like the dummy could not be found, traders—especially Gypsy traders—were known to train horses, for example, to collapse on the ground whenever harness was put on them or upon the universal command "Giddap!" Or horses were deliberately taught to respond exactly opposite to commands. The dismayed buyer could be expected to complain and accept his old horse back—but without the boot money, which the trader accepted as tuition money for teaching the duped customer a very valuable lesson.

Indeed, the concept of back-trading is without question the most common theme in all horse trading stories throughout the United States, possibly because it was the most common dodge played by horse traders.

This next story carries the back-trading motif but is also richly embroidered with other themes, besides providing a good deal of background information about the horse trader, his life, and his philosophy of life.

The tale was collected from Joseph Pachunka of Fullerton, Nebraska, by F. A. Kiolbasa on 3 March 1940. Pachunka (and perhaps even Kiolbasa) must not have used standard English regularly. Unlike the other tales in this collection, this one has required substantial rewording of each sentence to make it intelligible.

One of the early day Polish pioneers in Nance County was Charles Augustine. He had come from Poland as a young man. There he had been a good, well-trained horseman and here he soon found that in trading horses one could make good money, if the trading was done in a good, business-like manner.

His way of dealing was always to give the other guy good advice while not actually pointing out any facts. He soon learned all of the trading tricks and thereby never hardly ever got left holding the bag. Sometimes he even came out of such deals with cash.

He always made a point of never carrying along a horse that he intended to keep for himself, that he did not mean to trade.

In the days when the county was new and new settlers were coming in, horses were in heavy demand and had to be brought in from other localities. Mr. Augustine soon was so established in the business that he went to other places where he could buy up horses by the carload, ship them in, and then go selling and trading. He knew every horse in his trading territory.

He would go out on buying trips, picking up animals however he could. Sometimes he would buy a whole herd of horses simply by pointing at them with his whip or riding through the herd. By buying in such a way he often came into possession of animals that were not even worth the transportation costs of returning them to his own place. But he never backed out on a deal—but on the other hand he always expected to get what had been promised him.

On one such occasion he bought a lot of horses and he got, among them, two iron gray mares, which he later found to be totally blind. But the mares were a perfectly matched pair and showed some real possibilities, so he culled the pair out of the herd, which he put under the trading hammer. He took the team for himself and would frequently hitch them up and taught them to drive nicely.

He was a good horseman and soon had the blind team trained so that they had all confidence in him when they were being driven, and he really showed them off. When he was sure that this team would not fail him when they were being driven, he drove them to Genoa [Nebraska], his best trading center. There he drove them up and down the streets in such a way as to show their best and not show that they were blind. When he was satisfied that they had been shown to their best advantage he tied the team to a hitching post so that they could be examined by anyone who wished.

His way was never to ask anyone for a trade but he would never refuse when someone else offered. Now, in a short time someone stopped him and offered another team in trade for this team of grays. Both of this man's team were sound, but they were not as well mated as the grays and did not drive as well.

When such trades were made there was no guarantee, but each man did look over the other man's horses very well. Mr.

104

Augustine said that he would have to have twenty-five dollars boot in such a trade, making it clear that any trade would be on an as-is basis. The deal was closed and Mr. Augustine got his twenty-five dollars. The men then took the horses to a local barn where the harness could be exchanged. Then each man drove out with his new team.

Now Augustine had warned the other man in front of witnesses to use good judgment in looking the team over, for "the team would not look at him."

After the harness had been changed, the men drove out into the street. Mr. Augustine got along well with the team he had received in the deal, but the other man was strange to the horses and was not handling them in the same way they had grown used to. The blind team came out of the barn and crowded the gate and nearly ran over their new owner. Only after he had them out and took another look did he realize that they were both blind.

Obviously he had not expected this and he felt that he had been cheated. But witnesses had heard Augustine say that he should look that team over pretty carefully because they would not look at him, so it was a fair deal.

The men back-traded however, Augustine taking back his blind team but keeping the twenty-five dollars boot. The team figured in many such deals for Mr. Augustine and in time brought more in boot cash than the full value of such teams even when they were sound.

Croughan's Puller

The next story underlines the contrary nature of the horse world. But despite the most powerful drives of my inner self, I cannot but see in this story about a singular horse the very essence of mankind. The Federal Writers Project files contain no documentation whatever for this tale, but its style suggests that it came from Lew Croughan and was therefore collected by Harold J. Moss.

One horse I traded for seemed perfectly sound. But I should have been suspicious because the farmer I traded with had a fixed grin on his face that looked as if he was going to break into a laugh any minute. He kept telling me what a puller his horse was. I soon found after the trade that the horse was a good puller, as the farmer had said, only all the pulling was done in reverse. The horse was one of those animals that pull back on the harness instead of pulling on the load. I had the horse hitched to the back of the wagon where, because of his trick of pulling back, he nearly upset the wagon several times. This kind of a horse is always an infernal nuisance, so I began wondering what to do with him. In addition to having a balky horse on my hands, I also had to worry about the wind, which was blowing such a gale that it threatened to tear off my wagon cover.

After traveling a short distance there was a jerk that I first thought was the wind, but it was my new horse. He had pulled back again and was hanging on the rope. Then, at the same time, there was a furious blast of wind that sailed off my wagon cover. It lighted on the balky horse, enveloping him as if it had been a strait jacket. He got his feet tangled until he was as helpless as if he had been roped. He just stood there and trembled, but he was quick to ease up on the rope. Because of the strong wind I had a devil of a time getting the canvas off from him.

When I finally got the thing loose, the horse crowded up to the end of the wagon and stood there with a scared look in his eyes. He never pulled back again while I had him, though he wasn't afraid of the canvas cover itself. He apparently thought I had used the canvas as a punishment for his pulling back.

Trading according to Hoyle

The introductory line to Jason Hoyle's horse stories might just as well be the watchword and epitaph of every horse trader who ever walked the earth and cheated his fellow man. Never had I seen the whole philosophy and rationale of swapping so neatly tied up in a single linguistic bundle. The material was collected from Hoyle by J. Willis Kratzer on 3 April 1941.

I was broke in early as a lad to take the world as I found it and not resort to crying. Horse trading in the early days was quite an art and the quicker a fellow learned to take care of himself, the better he was prepared to meet life squarely. I was only a boy when I took the notion that I wanted a pony, and why not, since every boy in the neighborhood who amounted to anything had one, and without a pony a fellow was pretty apt to remain by his lonesome through the many years to come, for the girls fell for the chap with the finest horseflesh to pull her hither and thither.

Now, Campin was not a regular horse trader, but like all farmers in the country he was pretty good at the art, for alike they had learned through experience with men who came regularly to take all to a cleaning who had not the training by past blunders.

Since Campin was a neighbor I thought I was safe in buying from him a pony which looked every bit a real buy for the money. To my sorrow I soon found that that pretty pony was the personification of every demon in Hades. He knew every trick a horse could master. He would balk, fight, kick, bite, rear in the harness, and about everything else, and not least among his ailments was that of snorting at every weed along the road like it was a demon in hiding.

I did everything which I knew to break him to act like an intelligent beast ought to, but it was all to no avail, and I found that I had taken a skinning at the hands of our neighbor Campin to the tune of about a hundred berries.

107

I swore that I would get even with him if it took me a hundred years, but the chance came about ten years later. I traded him a standard breed black for a gray team. It came about like this.

I had the horse, which was a beauty, in the barn and Campin came to our place. I purposely led that big black out to water and Campin, knowing that I had no mate for it, soon inquired what I wanted in trade.

I informed him that I didn't want a trade and that I had bought him to drive single, and he sure was a stepper—which he was—and I didn't lie a bit. He was as fine as ever was driven on the road.

Campin became more interested. I just took the horse to him and let him rub its nose and look it over, all the time saying that a trade was out of the question, but of course I had no objection to a neighbor admiring my horse flesh. I suggested that the fellows in town would be jerked off their high perch when I called for my girl with that black hitched to the buggy.

Campin was caught off guard. Besides, I was just a young fellow and not supposed to know any trading gags. He desired earnestly that I make him a proposition. Finally I said that if he wanted that black so bad, he should be willing to trade two for one—and demanded the fine team of grays he was driving.

He scratched his head and called it a hard bargain, but it seems that he had wanted a black for a long time, and this I knew, so I made it first, last, and only—take it or leave it—two grays for my black.

Campin took me up after much rag chewing and took the black away and left the grays.

When I saw him in town a few days later he did not speak to me, and this continued for a couple of years. Now, the truth is there were not men enough in the country to lead that black through a barn door. He would plunge and snort at every door, and, unless held with a chain, would break his harness all to bits. Reckon he was just plain door shy. Everywhere else he was worth his weight in gold.

A couple of years later I brought myself to climb Campin about the matter and ask him if it wasn't time to bury the

108

hatchet since he had given me a skinning several years previous, and I had skinned him a couple of years back, which made things about even. And I thought that we should forget it and be friends again—but not horse trading friends. It was agreed, and after that we were friends but did no more trading. We remained friends.

In my trading I picked up another brute. It was a big work horse, black with a star, and in good flesh. Looked like a million dollars.

But that horse was balky like nobody's business. I made up my mind that I would make him go, so I put a log chain over his back and down between his front legs, and hitched a team on in front and pulled the living daylights right out of him. That chain over his back must have hurt like sin, for he went like a good fellow.

The next time he balked I threw the chain over his back, and he started without waiting for me to hitch another team in front of him. After that, all I did was rattle a chain which I always had with me.

I got tired of that and finally decided to sell him. He would drive single, and as long as there was a chain handy to rattle he went along without any trouble and was pretty as a picture when he was driven alone.

I took him to Haymarket Square [in Lincoln] and a fellow wanted him for his wife. I didn't want to sell, of course, for no one ever wanted to trade or sell. It didn't pay. I let the fellow know that I prized that horse very highly and "couldn't a fellow come to Lincoln to buy some plug tobaccer without everybody thinking that he wanted to sell his horse?"

Finally he begged me to set a price. I said that I wouldn't consider a red cent less than one hundred and fifty dollars, take it or leave it quick, for I ought to have the seat of my pants kicked for even making that proposition.

He chewed his tongue a little but took the deal. As he climbed into his buggy I rattled the chain a little, which I had in my overcoat, it being a chain taken from a wagon, just a little one used to hold the two sides of the box from spreading. The horse started off swell and took him home.

In a few days I saw him again and he implored me to tell him how to make that horse go. He begged that I should come and show the wife how to start him.

I reached for my pocket and took out the little chain which I still had there and handed it to him, telling him to tell his wife to rattle it a little and that the horse would go forever. Each time it was hitched, just rattle the chain a little and that horse would travel as far as was desired.

The fellow was happy to find out the secret, although I think that he thought that he was skinned a little in the deal.

Horses and dogs have a lot in common. They both have an unusual amount of good sense for beasts. Take a dog I once had for instance. It was my habit to tie him every night before I went to bed, and I did this without fail for a long time.

Then there came a few times when he was out hunting or calling on friends and did not get home until past his usual hour and sure as shooting that dog came to the window where I was sleeping inside and scratched on the screen for me to come out and tie him up so he could sleep with a clear conscience.

Bargains

William R. Cole of Omaha provided the WPA files with a rambling series of short reminiscences and tales about his fifty years as a horse trader. He was born in 1870 and so had ample opportunity to trade during the final years when the horse was still the only mode of transportation and power across the land.

The report of A. E. Finch, the fieldworker who talked with Cole, gave the following sad description of the tough old horse trader's condition.

Pleasant, kindly face with soft, pleasing voice; has suffered a great deal of arthritis and hand and legs are badly crippled from this trouble. He moves around on heavy pads strapped around his

110

legs, *walking on his knees; feet so badly crippled has to wear soft house slippers and cannot walk on feet. Has bright outlook on life and hopes some day to again be able to go fishing and also to transact a few more horse trades before he has to give up entirely. Very cheery for his age and condition; enjoys talking to people and having them come and visit with him.*

Cole mentions a few cures for balky or reluctant horses, but the cures for such contrariness were legion. Pebbles, for example, were dropped into the horse's ears immediately before the trade began, and the potential buyer would see a horse briskly prancing and shaking its head as if full of vinegar and just raring to go. Pebbles, however, seldom effected a permanent cure for a balky horse!

Or, on the other hand, wads of cotton were soaked in chloroform and jammed up the animal's nostrils shortly before the bargaining so that the horse stood there just as calm and quiet as anyone could desire for his wife's buggy. In essence, of course, the man was buying a sleeping horse, and once the horse woke up, the duped buyer also woke up.

A second point worth noting is Cole's mention of the eminent desirability of a matched team. For one thing, a well-matched team could be worth a full one hundred dollars more than a mixed set and so was very much sought after, but above all it was a matter of personal pride: a matched team made a handsome outfit and "would jerk the fellows off their high perch," as Jason Hoyle put it, when the driver went calling on his girl friend. Every man carried his pride on his horses, just as now a man's pride often is exhibited in his automobile.

In fact, a motif that frequently appears in horse folklore centers on this desire to sport a well-matched team. The tale tells of two men who are virtually possessed with the idea of finding a mate for a fine bay mare they jointly own. A smooth trader sees and seizes the opportunity by convincing the one man one Sunday that he will never find a mate for that mare and buys the horse, paying, however, a handsome price. But no matter: he quickly goes to the partner's house, shows him the animal—a perfect mate for the mare the man still believes he owns—and sells it to him for a far handsomer price, the buyer

111

now believing that he will have a fortune in the magnificently matched twins. The story usually ends with the trickster leaving town as abruptly as possible with his ill-gotten gains!

Finch collected the following material from William R. Cole on 21 November 1941.

Like thousands of other young Germans, my father fled Germany shortly before he became of age, to escape compulsory military training. Coming to America he married and settled near Fort Leavenworth, Kansas, where I was born on January 7, 1870. There were two boys and two girls in my family beside myself; the other two boys and one sister have passed on and I live with the other sister here in Omaha. When I was about school age I had the scarlet fever and it left me in such condition that I did not start school until I was thirteen. When I did start though, I entered the fourth grade and went right on from there; father had taught me a great deal before I was able to start school. He had a very good education, especially in mathematics and spelling. I don't think there was any word you could stump him on spelling.

I always liked horses from as early as I can remember and the same year I started school, when I was thirteen, I also started trading horses. I have been at it ever since until a few years ago when this arthritis took me. I have been so crippled up ever since I am unable to do anything. My father and mother were both killed in a streetcar accident or wreck on the Douglas Street Bridge in 1893.

I can remember back to about the time of the Custer Massacre. I think it was about 1876. A man by the name of Dave Redman was shipping the first saw mill to Deadwood, South Dakota. They had all the mill equipment loaded on wagons and hitched sixteen horses to each wagon. The people and supplies were loaded in other wagons and these were hauled by ox teams. They expected a lot of trouble from the Indians—that would be the Sioux tribe they would run up against—but they made the trip without any trouble. When they were loading up, Redman told father to load a barrel of syrup on one of the wagons so if they met up with any

112

troublesome Indians they could just roll the barrel off and leave it. That would settle the entire matter right then. Everyone thought that was a funny thing to pacify the Indians with.

There are several different kinds of horse traders. There's the roving Gypsies, the white road traders who keep traveling from place to place, trading along the road as they go, and then there's the barn trader, one who usually operates from a barn or livery stable, maybe one he owns himself or one from which he works with another owner.

I ran a livery barn on the northwest corner of Twentieth and Ohio Streets [in Omaha] at one time; right next to it stood the Lone Tree Hotel. A man by the name of Folsom ran the hotel and he was a brother of Mrs. Grover Cleveland, wife of the one-time president.

Another livery barn I used to own and run was known as the Club Stables and stood on Capitol Avenue between Tenth and Seventeenth Streets. In those days all this part of the city up here around Fortieth Street was good fertile farm land. We didn't have any automobiles in those days. When you wanted to get around the city or put on a little dog, you hired a hack. Every good livery barn had from one to three hacks, some of the larger ones had more. The drivers usually worked on commission. Some of them were pretty hard drinkers too.

In those days, when your wealthier people went downtown shopping, it wasn't so much to see what was in the stores or to buy something as it was to show off their fine horses and carriages and to attract attention. People in those days took a great deal of pride in their horses and carriages, with their spiffy coachmen and possibly a coach dog either riding with them or trotting along under the carriage.

I made a lot of money trading horses during my life and had a lot of fun too as I went along. I can't remember all the exact dates as I never paid any particular attention to them at the time, but I'll tell you some of the experiences I had.

One time I had an old sorrel hack horse which I just couldn't get rid of around here. Everyone knew him too well. One day I thought I would drive over to Council Bluffs and see what I could do. While crossing the bridge I met one of those

113

road traders. I spotted him before I got to him—you can always tell them as far as you can see them when you have been in the game awhile. He hailed me with "Pull up there, Mister. Maybe we can make a deal."

He wanted to trade me a poor looking horse that still had its long winter coat of hair on. After considerable arguing I swapped with him and took my new horse home and put him in the barn. When I tried to take him out I found he wouldn't back. I had to get a team of horses and pull him out of the stall. Another thing, he would bite anyone who came near him.

Well, all this didn't bother me. I got a pair of clippers and slicked him up til he looked like seven hundred dollars, put some racing plates on his feet, hitched him to a racing buggy, and started out. I remember some of those road traders used to hang out around Twenty-first and Paul Streets, so I headed for that vicinity.

As I drove past one of them yelled at me but I just kept on going. About two hours later I drove back that same way and this time he got out in the road and stopped me. Asked me if I wanted to sell that horse, and I told him no, he was too good a horse. He argued around for a while and I finally decided to trade for a dandy good team of mules he had. He wanted me to leave the horse right then but I told him I would have to take the buggy home and lead the mules behind but that I would send the horse right back. I got home with my mules and had a boy hide them out in a lot and sent him back with the horse.

It wasn't long before the boy came back, half scared, and told me that I had better get ready for a visit because that horse had bitten the man almost as soon as he got him there. My friend, the road trader, showed up all right in due time but he wasn't mad; he came to congratulate me. You see, he was the man on the bridge. He only found out that he had been paid in his own change when that horse bit him.

On another occasion I heard there were some good horses near Tekamah [Nebraska] for sale, so I went up there and after dickering around for a while I bought three of them for two hundred dollars. They were mighty nice horses, any one of them worth what I paid for the lot.

I started back for Millard and on the road I met the fire chief and sold him a nice bay for two hundred and eighty-five dollars. That was the standard price for a good fire horse. I still had the other two and had made eighty-five dollars in cash so far that day. I sold another one, a black, to Millard Miller here in Omaha for two hundred dollars in gold and a balky horse. This balky fellow I sold to a farmer. I told him the horse was balky but he liked the looks of him and said that he would soon break him of that. He wanted me to stay all night, which I finally did.

He had the horse down at the far side of a lot and he wouldn't budge an inch. The farmer brought a big cart down and hitched him to it, filled the cart up with big heavy rocks and stones and left him there with it. The cart was loaded until it would have been a good pull for a team of horses. During the night a big electrical storm and rain came up and it just poured.

The next morning when we went out to the barn that horse was standing there neighing to get in the barn. He had dragged that cartload of stone through the rain and mud clear across that lot to the barn. The farmer unhitched him, put him in the barn, rubbed him down, and fed him. Later he hitched him up with another horse to a wagon and that balky horse was the first one in the collar to pull. He never balked again; he was cured.

At another time I had a big black horse that I had paid seventy-five dollars for. He was balky too. He would get his tongue over the bit of the bridle and you couldn't do a thing with him. We tried taping his mouth and tongue down so he couldn't get it over the bit but that didn't help. He would just rear up on his hind legs and refuse to budge.

I said, "Okay, Mister, I'll fix you." We hitched another horse up with him, gave him a drink, tied the other horse to a tree and went away and left him. That evening I tried them out and he wouldn't move. We changed the other horse and hitched another with him and left them all night.

The next morning the same thing, not a move out of him. We again changed the other horse, gave him a drink, and left

115

them standing there all day. That night the same thing over again.

We repeated the changes with a fresh horse and more water for him and left them the second night. The next morning we tried them. He stepped right off. He was getting so hungry, having stood there so long, that he was willing to go in order to eat and have a chance to rest.

That horse was cured too. You can't whip it out of a horse. Abuse makes them all the meaner and harder to handle, but you can break their stubborn will or spirit, or whatever you want to call it.

One day I heard of a man at Fremont who had a horse to sell, one that would match up with one I already had, so I drove up there. I inquired where he lived and when I drove up to the place I inquired if he had any pigs or stock hogs to sell.

He said he didn't, whereupon I told him I guessed I must have been misinformed and asked if he knew of any. He might have told me no and closed up with that but luckily he said he had a horse he would like to sell.

I let on as though I was no more than mildly interested and asked the price. He wanted a hundred and twenty-five dollars for it. I asked to see it and he showed it to me, offered to hitch it up and take a drive. I told him to go ahead and hitch it up but just a couple blocks would be far enough. He did and drove the horse back hard to show his wind was okay. I offered him seventy-five dollars for it; he held out for a hundred twenty-five, but I stalled.

He went back and talked to his wife sitting on the porch. They talked in German, not knowing that I understood every word they said. She told him to hold out for the hundred and twenty-five dollars but not to lose the sale. Finally I gave in to one hundred dollars if he would come down to that figure, which he did, and we closed the deal.

If you want to get a good bargain, never be too anxious or in a hurry. Stall and jew on the price asked. You can always get it for less than they ask in the first place. Note, I asked for hogs, not horses. That led him to think I bought the horse because I thought I was getting a bargain, and I was too, for I sold the team at a very handsome profit. In fact, I had the team sold for several weeks before I bought the last horse. All I had to do was find the match for the one I had and they matched up perfectly.

I never did care very much for running races or horses. I like a good trotter or pacer best. I think the nicest race is a cart or sulky race. One time I had a nice mare and two colts and I knew a fellow who had a pacer I would like to own. I had seen the horse a lot of times so hit him for a deal. He made the deal all right and when I went to get the pacer I found it was in charge of a veterinary, a Dr. Blackwell, and he had the horse strung up in slings. The animal's muscles had been strained and he told me it would take about six weeks before I could take it home. You see, I took it for granted the horse was all right. I had seen it a lot of times and was sure I knew what I was getting. I didn't ask about it and the man didn't tell me, so I took it as is. He paid the doctor's bill and I paid for the keep and care of the horse until it got all right, so I came out all right on that deal.

In horse trading or any other kind of trading, it isn't always a case of misrepresenting your stock or wares; it's just a case of being as foxy as the other fellow, or maybe a little better. The best of them get stung sometimes and I was no exception. But you just want to be smart enough to get rid of your bargains.

One time I bought a milk cow and calf for one dollar. She was an old bob-tail white cow and I found out she didn't give over a pint of milk and the calf was sucking that. She was more of the beef type than the milking strain. I didn't have much invested but the next thing was to get rid of my poor investment to advantage. I found a Swede that had a lazy horse and I hit him for a trade.

I offered him a milk cow and a calf with twenty-five dollars cash for his horse. He took the deal up right then and I delivered the cow and calf and took my horse home.

In a couple of days there was one mad Swede called on me. He stormed around a while but finally was convinced it was his own fault. I didn't say how much milk the cow gave and he didn't ask me. I sold him a milk cow; she was giving milk and that was all there was to it. He couldn't do a thing about it.

I knew horses, both good ones and poor ones. I have bought a lot of horses for the fire department here, but in the days before they motorized everything. I never tried to gyp them. I knew what they wanted and they knew that I would get it for them. I have made several trips to Kentucky and bought up some of their fine carriage horses for Omaha's elite in the horse and carriage days. Sometimes I have paid two hundred dollars each for such horses, plus the shipping expense of getting them back here.

One time I saw a beautiful animal in South Omaha. He had a white coat with black spots about the size of a quarter all over him. The spots were the most even size I ever saw. I bought him for seventy-five dollars and he was only four years old.

One day I was passing the Grand Hotel and a fellow saw him. He had one that was almost the exact mate to him and he wanted to sell him. He asked a good, big price to start with, but I wasn't overly interested, at least not that I let him know of, but I was just itching to get that horse of his, for I knew where I could sell the team in five minutes.

I finally got him down to one hundred dollars and I snapped it up right then. I had one hundred and seventy-five dollars in that team. I slicked them up until they just shone and took them around to my prospect. We took a ride, he drove them, liked them, and give me a check for two thousand dollars for that team without a quibble. You see how you can make money trading horses or knowing how to buy? That was eighteen hundred and twenty five dollars right there, as much as some fellows made working all year in those days, and I had made it in a few days' time.

Oh, I got beat a lot of times too, just as well as others did, but I always watched my change and got rid of my bad bargains with as little loss as possible, if any at all.

The Good-as-Gold Gelding

The unidentified narrator of this tale exhibits all the symptoms of the terminally infected horse trader. Even though he knows that the horse in question cannot be the bargain it seems—it must have some hidden and horrible fault—he proceeds with the trade anyway. The defrauded horse trader then applies the kind of logic best understood by both traders and horses, which, predictably, does not work.

One morning in the middle '60's I was approached by a shiftless trader, known as "Ripgut," who always had a large string of half-starved trading stock around. He got his name from his seasonal habit of cutting slough grass (known as ripgut) with which to feed his bony plugs.

On this day he showed up with a fair looking gelding. The horse wasn't beautiful to look at, being a dirty gray, but was unusually smooth and well fed for coming from Ripgut's stock. At that I wouldn't have paid any attention to Ripgut or his horse if I hadn't had a brown mare I wasn't too keen about.

Ripgut started talking trading in a big way. "In this horse," he said, "you will find a good rider and worker that is sound as a United States of America dollar." I knew the horse couldn't have all the perfections Ripgut claimed for him, but he looked good enough for a trade.

Well, that horse turned out to be worse than I had ever thought it possible for any horse to be. Most horses, even the very bad ones, have only one nasty trick but this horse knew the whole book. He was a balker, would sit down, lay down, walk backwards, and kick. I didn't know any one horse could have so much cussedness in him.

But I made up my mind to do something with this gray if it was nothing else than to shoot him. So I started working him, but the work turned into a battle of wits between the two of us, with the horse usually on the winning side.

119

He was as peaceful as a dove when I first hitched him to the wagon, but the moment I took up the reins and began driving he balked. Then, to make matters worse, he turned his head around in a high-hatted manner, to see what I was going to do about it. Finally I got him to moving but only until we came to the top of a hill, where he came to a dead stop for the apparent purpose of looking over the country. After a considerable delay he began moving again. Then, after we had traveled a mile or so he decided to lay down. This time I hit him with the whip, which, instead of making him behave, caused him to walk backwards until the rear of the buggy was pushed against a tree.

I was now good and mad, so again reached for my whip. I wound the lash around my arm and hit him over the ear with the loaded stock. The blow stunned him enough to bring him down on his knees. Apparently he had had enough; he didn't create any more trouble that day.

The third time he balked was on the section line west of Central City [Nebraska] when he just stopped and refused to move. He didn't sit or lie down as he had done previously. Again I reached for my whip, but before I could hit him he had pushed the buggy backwards into a ditch, after which he had pulled out as rapidly as he could, apparently with the idea of throwing me out of the wagon. Fortunately I had a good hold on the seat or he would have succeeded. The old boy was learning new tricks. He must have worked all night thinking out this new one.

I didn't have any more trouble for a week. Then, one evening when we were hitting it off for home in a light buggy, one of our local dandies pulled up beside us with a spanking outfit and started to pass. My cuss of a horse immediately saw red and would have raced if I hadn't held him down to let the other fellow get around. He didn't like it a bit, and I too sort of hated to hold him back. It was an insult to his running abilities. Besides, there was something about his determined spirit I liked.

As the buggy passed us he ceased being insulted and became mad. The first thing he did was to stop dead, after

120

which he lifted his heels over the single tree and trace in preparation to letting go with both feet on his target, which was the dashboard. The best I could do in the face of his attack was to crawl out of the buggy at the rear just as he kicked a hole in the dashboard and ripped the back cushion of the seat into shreds. If I had remained in my original position I would have been killed.

The horse then gracefully pulled his legs back in the shafts, after which he turned around to survey the damage. A mischievous gleam was in his eyes, but I didn't do or say anything as I crawled back on the seat. In a minute we were on our way as if nothing had happened.

Yes, that horse was unique. But he went the way of all horse trading horses. I traded him for a filly who became wind-broke after any extra effort.

Part III: *SOME TRADES*

Tricks of the Trade

Horses that do not balk or kick or refuse to back up or refuse to go forward, horses that do not display some personality disorder are certain to have any of a myriad of disabling, momentarily invisible, and incurable ailments.

To the city dweller's ear the names are strange or even humorous—founders, lampers, botts, fistula, lump jaw, splint, stifle joint, poll-evil, sweenies, and scours, for example. And the cures were frequently stranger than the ailments, some examples of which you have seen in previous stories. Among some other cures that were touted as effective on the pioneer Plains, as cited in my Treasury of Nebraska Pioneer Folklore:

> (for botts): Drench the horse with tea made from tobacco. Cut off his tail.
>
> (for lampers): Grease the horse's tail and croup with old bacon rind and grease.
>
> (for stifle joint): Let the horse stand in a creek for 24 hours.
>
> (for scours): ... Bind the horse's tail about six inches from the root. Use a stout cord or hair from the horse's tail and let it stay bound not longer than four hours.
>
> Or by way of general treatment, "After a horse has been castrated, pull the horse's tail three times and the horse will never die."

The general public was not, however, totally at the mercy of the traders. The People's Home Library, by R. C. Barnum, for example, gave all manner of advice in etiquette, cookery, home medicine, and animal care and included three pages of specific things to watch for when trading horses. The tricks Barnum warns against are precisely those we have seen played by the unscrupulous on the unwary in these pages:

During my thirty years of experience, I have had occasion to buy and sell several thousand horses and have met with a great many deceptions among unscrupulous horse traders. I have assisted in sending several crooked horse dealers to the state's prison and for the protection of the public, I have deemed it wise to expose a few of their tricks. Beware the Tricks of Horse Swindlers.

1. **Dieting and Doping a Heaver.**—Broken winded horses breathe easier when empty, hence bulky food is kept from them, their food is dampened with lime water and they are doped with such drugs as arsenic, lobelia, chloral hydrate, opium, stramonium or even lard or linseed oil and sometimes bird shot is given them to palliate or hide the symptoms of heaves until the horse is unloaded on the purchaser.

   Caution to Buyer.—Let him eat his fill of dry, bulky food or satisfy his thirst with water, then trot him up a hill or on a muddy road or otherwise subject him to violent exercise and he will show the symptoms of heaves.

2. **Plugging a Roarer or Whistler.**—It is a common practice to insert a sponge in one or both nostrils with thread attached, making it possible to clear the nostril after the sale is made. Or, sometimes both ends are cut from a lemon, it is squeezed dry and then inserted in the nostril where it will shrink and be blown out later by the horse. Plugging the nostrils prevents roaring or whistling for the time being. Checking the head high also aids in covering up the symptoms.

   Caution to Buyer.—Always examine high up in nostrils when buying a horse. Also give him a brisk gallop to bring out the symptoms.

3. **Blowing Up Old and Sweenied Horses.**—When a dishonest horse trader has a sweenied horse, it is a common practice for him to blow air under the skin over the shrunken parts. He does this by puncturing the skin and blowing air under it through a tube or goose quill. This gives the wasted parts the appearance of being normal. Sometimes

126

this is done with old horses to give them a younger appearance.

Caution to Buyer.—By applying pressure to the parts with the hand a crackling noise is produced which is quite unnatural, therefore by close observation this trick is easily discovered.

4. **Paralyzing a Switcher.**—Unscrupulous dealers, to stop switching and "line grabbing" until after a sale is made, hang a four or five pound weight to the tail for several hours or tie the tail up over the back, keeping it in a fixed position until the tail is temporarily paralyzed. This prevents switching while the partial paralysis lasts.

Caution to Buyer.—It is always suspicious when a horse hangs the tail in a limp or pendulous way and never moves or switches it.

5. **Gingering.**—Crooked horse traders frequently insert a piece of ginger root in the lower bowel or moisten the anus with an irritating medicine of some kind to make him carry a high tail and act more lively when in the show ring or on the road.

Caution to Buyer.—Be suspicious when a horse carries his tail too high.

6. **Hiding Lameness.**—Horse swindlers have learned to handle the hypodermic syringe and inject cocaine over the nerves on each side of a lame leg. This prevents pain and makes the horse go sound until after a sale or trade is consummated.

Frequently they have a section of the nerve taken out and this permanently relieves the animal of pain below the fetlock. Sometimes the nerve is severed or divided above the knee or hock and this relieves lameness below.

Often the shoe is pulled off the foot of lame leg to deceive the buyer into believing that the lameness was caused by casting a shoe and is only temporary.

Caution to Buyer.—Watch closely for scars or needle

punctures, especially above and below the fetlock. Be suspicious of a lame horse that has cast a shoe.

7. **Hiding Spavins, Ringbones and Sidebones.**—Unscrupulous horse dealers frequently make wounds or skin abrasions over a spavin, ringbone or sidebone, or they bruise the parts to produce local swelling. This sometimes misleads the buyer into believing that the horse has met with a recent and trivial injury from which he will soon recover.

Caution to Buyer.—Hesitate to buy a horse when suffering from a wound or skin abrasion in the localities where these blemishes are found.

8. **Putting Harness Galls on a Balky Horse.**—Gypsies and disreputable horse traders very often burn sores on the shoulders and disarrange the hair on top of the horse's neck as though caused by a collar. They also chafe the horse's sides as though done by the harness. This is done to make the innocent purchaser believe that the horse received these scars while doing hard work in the harness while it is possible that the horse will not pull a pound in the harness.

Caution to Buyer.—Insist on seeing the horse work and pull a heavy load.

9. **"Doctoring" a Cribber.**—To conceal the fact that a horse is a cribber, horse traders sometimes saw between the incisor teeth or drive small wedges between them or make the mouth sore by cutting or burning the gums. The horse is not likely to crib while his mouth is very sore.

Caution to Buyer.—Examine the mouth and incisor teeth very carefully before buying.

10. **Winding a Horse.**—A common trick of horse traders when showing a broken winded horse is to gallop past the buyer, then go slow and consume as much time as possible in turning. This allows the horse to catch his wind and not show his broken wind when galloping past the buyer. Sometimes the horse is made to appear as though trying to run away and thus requiring to be held in. The head is also

128

checked high and the nose kept poked out as much as possible.

Caution to Buyer.—Insist on the horse being galloped fast for a considerable distance and the nose pulled well into the breast.

11. **"Bishoping."**—For nearly a hundred years gypsies and dishonest horse traders have been known to "Bishop" the teeth, thus making an old horse appear young to the casual observer. The operation consists in cutting cups in the table surface and staining them with nitrate of silver, thereby giving the old tooth the appearance of a much younger one. Special tools are made for this purpose and it is astonishing how expert some of the horse traders become in this art.

Caution to Buyer.—An old horse seldom has the appearance of a young one, and the teeth have an entirely different appearance. The difference can readily be noticed upon comparison.

12. **The "Stool-Pigeon Swindler."**—In all large cities, it is common practice with many disreputable horse dealers to advertise a horse as being the property of Mrs. Blank, who is represented to the customer as a widow. She, of course, is always dressed in black and sheds tears with ease while in reality she is the "stool-pigeon" or accomplice of the swindler. Various misrepresentations are made and after the swindle is discovered by the purchaser he is either unable to find the sellers or he finds them to be irresponsible parties from whom no damages can be collected. I have known operators of this kind to rent as many as six or eight barns in various parts of the city and advertise a horse first at one and then at another.

Caution to Buyer.—Beware of "stool-pigeons" and widows (when buying horses) and have a doubt in your mind when answering advertisements of this kind. Don't be influenced by the horse stories of strangers but buy the horse on its merits.

13. **Matching a Fractious Horse with a Lazy One.**—To deceive innocent purchasers, dishonest dealers sometimes dope an unmanageable horse with drugs to make him quiet and gentle. Or, sometimes the horse is walked or driven, before shown for sale, until he is nearly exhausted. These things are also done to match a fractious horse with a quiet, lazy one and make them travel well together.

    Caution to Buyer.—In matching horses never decide too quickly and especially if the animal impresses you as being vicious or excitable for he may have been "fixed" to deceive you.

14. **The Straw and Stringhalt Trick.**—When horses show stringhalt the trader very often accounts for it by saying it is a habit contracted on account of being bedded deeply in rye straw, thus obliging the horse to lift his feet high while walking about the box stall.

    Caution to Buyer.—Don't accept an excuse or apology for an ailment of this kind. The excuse is generally made of "straw."

15. **The Dark Trick.**—Horse traders frequently desire to dispose of horses that are suffering from moon blindness (periodic ophthalmia) and this is an incurable eye defect which is much worse at some times than others. These horses are usually disposed of in the evening or at the time when they show the defect the least.

    Caution to Buyer.—Never buy a horse in the dark. Notice that both eyes are the same size, and that the lids are normal and the eyeballs transparent and not of a bluish color.

16. **Stuffing the Ears.**—The ears of nervous and excitable horses are often stuffed with cotton, wool or oakum to render the animal deaf and thus prevent his becoming frightened by noise.

    Caution to Buyer.—Always examine both ears closely.

130

17. **The Meaning of Many Scars.**—Scars are frequently the result of runaways or falling during a fit. The animal may be unmanageable or subject to blind staggers or the scars may have been produced by injuries received while rolling and tumbling with frequent attacks of colic.

    Caution to Buyer.—Beware of a horse with many scars unless you know what caused them.

Ailing Horses and a Sick Owner

But traders as often as not were interested only in cosmetic applications, anything that would make a horse look better for the duration of the trading negotiations regardless of the ultimate damage that cure might cause later. So, for example, arsenic and cocaine play a major role in the following stories and some of those above.

Lew Croughan could be compassionate with other traders, as we have seen in previous stories, and he was very soft-hearted when it came to his horses. Not only did he not abuse his animals, but it upset him when others were unkind or thoughtless to theirs. Late in 1940, fieldworker Harold Moss asked Croughan about horses' diseases and ailments and the methods used by traders to cure or cover them.

Lots of things happen to horses and a horse trader makes it his business to know the various defects and ailments and the remedy, if any. A stifled horse is often, or was, familiar to many people and to all horse handlers. Today it is doubtful if one out of a hundred average people know what it is or have even heard about it for that matter.

    A stifled horse is one whose coffin joint, just below the hip joint, becomes unbuckled. It often results from stepping on the feet under heavy draft. It causes him, when trailing, to hitch on that leg and drag the point of the hoof. About the only

131

remedy for a stifle is to shoe that hoof with most of the steel in the toe of the shoe. However, it is a hard defect to cover up and a trader cannot do much about it except to use them as the cheapest of trading stock.

A horse's hoof is made up of many bones and parts and since it supports the weight of the body, a thousand pounds or more, and transmits the motive and tractive power, it is subject to terrific strains, blows, and pressures. It is little wonder that a horse goes lame now and then and, nine times out of ten, it is caused by a nail or thorn in the soft part or quick of the hoof. There is another cause of lameness, however, which is not so simple to correct as a nail in the tender part, and that is when a horse comes "hoof bound."

This condition is generally brought about by hard driving on hard roads or rocky fields. The heel of the hoof becomes contracted and the substance above the frog inflamed.

The only cure I know of for this is to shoe that foot with a spring steel shoe held together by a temporary clasp. It is necessary to attach this shoe with two extra nails. When it is nailed in place the clasp then can be removed and the shoe expands. This action spreads the hoof and allows the frog more freedom to come back to its proper place. Generally it works but not always.

A good horse trader, you see, not only employs temporary remedies but also endeavors to bring about a permanent correction of defects. Farmers, who use most of the horses used, are notorious for knowing very little about them. But I always made them believe they were wizards when it came to horse science.

"Well, well," I used to tell them, "don't that beat all! I've been handling horses of all kinds for years and I never heard that before." Then he would look wise and tell me something that I'd known for years. Of course they spread it on thick at times with some pretty fantastic ideas, but at least a few of them taught me things I didn't know.

A moon-eyed horse is supposed to go blind in the light of the moon and according to my best observation some horses do have that trouble. An experienced horseman always looks into

132

a horse's eyes but he is usually just looking for eye spots, which sometimes result in total blindness. A horse said to be moon-eyed has a dim, bleary eye.

Most horses go blind from eye injuries of some kind and a small, milky growth starts up and eventually spreads across the whole eye. Horse traders and owners could often take off those spots by blowing burnt alum or sugar through a quill into the horse's eyes.

The horse was one of man's best friends and without their pioneering, building up a new country would have been a slow and difficult job. Being a horseman it may be that I am too radical on the subject but it hurts me to know how many horse owners treat their aged stock. Greed, of course, is at the bottom of the whole thing. Up to the beginning of the mad machine age along in the early 1900's those who owned and used horses had some regard for them when they were too old to do any hard work. After working the daylights out of them for ten to twenty years it was right and proper that the old horses be pensioned off and kept around in order that they might have the reward of a well-earned rest before they passed on.

I've seen some sights which filled me with disgust for some of man's brutality and greed. As they became crazed over machinery they turned on their old friends, the horses, and murdered them, just to save a few dimes.

One time I recall feed was high and horses cheap and farmers took perfectly good horses out and shot them for hog feed and then turned around and paid out two and three thousand dollars for automobiles and tractors.

I have one case in mind which was positively revolting to me. You see, I come to know a good many farmers over the territory and their horses too. One in particular up in Burt Country [Nebraska] had quite a string of horses and he did all right by them until his head got full of little tractors and high-powered machinery.

He had one mare, a splendid piece of horse flesh, who had raised him twenty-seven head, besides giving him years of hard work. She was old when I last saw her, something over thirty years, I'd say. I always admired that mare; she had

133

helped make her owner rich. Being in the vicinity I decided to stop in and see this farmer and also the mare, for she was really an extraordinary horse. Her name I even knew too; it was Bessie.

Well, just as I drove into the yard, here come one of his half-grown boys, leading Bessie out of the barn. As I drew up I saw my farmer friend out by the hog lot, a rifle resting against a post. I thought he was preparing to butcher and he was, all right, but not a hog. He didn't pay any attention to me but called to the boy to bring Bessie to the hog lot, which the kid did.

It struck me cold what he was up to, and I called over to him to hold up a bit and maybe I could make a deal for his mare. I would have paid him ten dollars for her and turned her out in my own lot. But he just gave me a fishy look and before I could even get down from the wagon he raised his gun and shot that faithful old mare through the head. It was a sickening sight to see her, after all those years, die that way, and I turned away as she for a moment stood rigid from the shock of the bullet and then collapsed.

I couldn't help but tell that farmer what I thought about it. He just stood there and laughed and then he had the gall to say, "Friend Croughan, that there was a hard job for me to do but times is hard and money close, and I just couldn't naturally keep my head above water without cuttin' down expenses. I'm near bankrupt."

He was, as near as I knew, worth about seventy-five thousand dollars. That is a fair example of what is going on everywhere now with horses and humans too.

The Most Amazing Case of Buttons

However, Croughan was not slow to patch up horses for quick trades or to do some funny manipulating in trades with dam-

aged animals. Nor were all of his customers apparently prepared to accept the altering of horse flesh as a standard practice or a part of the trading game. The introduction of the legal system into the trade described in the next story reminds me of a passage I once read in Earl Conrad's Horse Trader. *A wily trader was explaining to Mrs. Conrad, Earl's mother, why precisely the formal legal system has no place whatever in the world of hoss swoppin':*

> Now you're raisin' a delicate point o' law, Missus, They's a lots of laws on the books about hoss *racin'* and hoss *stealin'*, but the whole danged business community has joined forces in seein' to it that there's practically no law allowed about buyin' and sellin' any kind of hoss one man is nervy enough to sell and another is foolish enough to buy. Furthermore, the jurisprudence of the thing don't rightly stake out any claims or limits on the how and why and whereas of said sales. Two traders can lick one if one chances to let two go to work on him; you can sell a mule for a hoss, if you're so minded and somebody else is so absent-minded to let it be done unto him; you can sell a dead hoss stuffed with straw if you can get away with it; you can go down to the boneyard and pick up the bones and put the bones together and get yourself a skeleton price on a belated hoss—if you can do it— and they ain't no law to prevent it. Hoss tradin', Ma'am, as you should know from the usufructs of your own husband's activities along this here line knows no bounds top nor bottom, side nor hind, and a common law among traders has so far agreed *not to have no law*. You work with your word, a paper in black and white, or your promises, or your downright story tellin' and the next man just takes his chance. [P. 124]

Perhaps the Dutchman of Croughan's next tale wound up learning that lesson in hoss tradin' law even if he did lose his case in court.

Horses have lots of ailments, but button farsee is one that generally isn't generally well known. It's a sort of growth on the skin of a horse's legs and belly which resembles buttons and sometimes their arrangement is in fairly straight lines, like buttons. The area around each "button" becomes sore and raw and in appearance it looks like wire cuts. One might take it to be wire cuts, although that would probably be far fetched. In the genuine disease the hair on the buttons or blisters turns white and the horse gants up.

Well, I learned that the same effect could be produced by applying spots of croton oil to a horse's belly and legs. The button-like lumps will appear quickly with this trick but much of the soreness is absent and there are no after affects. It is possible, with a swab, to attain a startling affect, such as straight lines, evenly spaced buttons and symmetrical patterns, which will mystify and bewilder anyone who isn't familiar with the trick.

I had a steel gray horse weighing about thirteen hundred pounds, which wasn't so bad though his head was a little pudgy. However, he wasn't worth much to me and I ran across a fellow who had a big brown mule he wanted to trade off for a horse of some kind.

He was an excitable Dutchman and big as a barrel, being about the same shape. Off hand, I would have taken him as being a little inclined to violence on occasion, but I was interested in a trade and paid no attention to that angle.

I wondered if there might be a chance to have a little fun with him and maybe more, so when I got ready to start over to see him I slipped a small bottle of croton oil in my pocket. He was a tough one to handle in a trade all right and after getting down to business, every few minutes he would waddle over to the house and call his wife out for consultation. I got tired of the delay but it gave me a chance to put a few drops of croton oil on the mule's belly and legs. I intended to fix my iron-gray up too but I wanted to be sure that the old boy would trade first. He wanted cash boot and I told him that I never paid out cash boot for mules.

Finally he said in his guttural mixed talk, "Shust you gebt me a writing dot your Pferde is alles gut aind vee swap, even, nicht wahr?"

I knew what he meant all right; he wanted a written guarantee with my horse. It didn't take me long to put him

136

straight on that. I just said, "You're a hell of a horse trader, asking for a written guarantee."

He understood perfectly and hurried into the house to get the last word from his "Frieda." I was pretty sure the deal was a go and this time I fixed my horse with the croton oil spots and it was the most artistic job of "buttons" anybody ever saw on a horse—straight rows and rings with a general pattern of flourishes that would make even a good horseman stick out his eyes when he saw the results.

We made the trade all right and I got away, taking his mule with me, while he led the iron-gray into his barn. There was no doubt in my mind but what there would be a mad Dutchman over to see me in a day or two when that croton oil got in its work. And sure enough, two days later I saw him driving up the road leading my iron-gray. He turned in, waving his arms and sputtering for me to follow and pointing to the horse's legs. He burst into a tirade of low German that I couldn't understand but could guess.

The iron-gray was a little stiff, but I didn't pay any attention to that. In fact, I just waited for the Dutchman to cool down a bit. He tumbled out of the wagon and shook his fist at me and trotted back to the iron-gray, gesturing for me to follow.

He had the most amazing imitation case of "buttons" I had ever seen. Rows and patterns of those bumps looked like they had been sewed on. The croton oil does take off a little hair or turns it white and they looked like the mill ends of hell under his belly and down the legs.

The Dutchman didn't seem to know what they were though I didn't expect him to know about the croton oil buttons. But he sure did know how to raise hell about it. I just let him go a while; he raved and ranted and cussed in high and low German and broken English. At first he was going to shoot me, as near as I could make out, then he threatened to have me arrested if I didn't give him back his mule. I just laughed at him and I thought he'd had a stroke.

Just to pacify him a little I said, "Those are just wire scratches. You let him get tangled up in the wire, and your old mule's got some of them too."

137

He quieted down a little at this and wanted to see the mule, which was in the yard back of the hay shed. Thinking he might try to recover the mule I kept an eye on him, but it was funny the way he gawked when he saw the "croton oil buttons" that studded the mule's legs. I said, "You can see your mule's in the same shape. Looks like wire scratches too."

But the old Dutchman was mad clear through and demanded that I pay him for his mule and take back my iron-gray. I decided to do it and offered him ten dollars. He just cussed in low German, most of which I didn't even understand. I could see that he was suspicious of the whole thing but he was scared to take his mule back or keep my horse. He thought it was a "Teufels Krankheit" ["devil's sickness"].

After a lot of heated haggling I give him twelve fifty and kept both animals, either one of which was worth seventy-five dollars in the right deal. The Dutchman drove away muttering threats about having me arrested, burning down my barn, and physical violence.

As soon as he was out of sight I made a mixture of acid vinegar and salt and fixed up both cases of the "buttons" and in a day or so there was nothing to show but light scars, about like wire scratches would leave, and a few white hairs.

I saw nothing more of that Dutchman for the time. And a few days later, in a three-way trade and sale I dealt off that iron-gray for what amounted to one hundred and twelve dollars and fifty cents, leaving me an even hundred dollars profit, figuring in the mule.

Some way or other the old boy heard something about it and he was so mad he made good his threat and had me arrested, charged with fraud, misrepresentation, and spreading disease, wilfully and maliciously. When the trial came up in court, the judge asked me what I thought was wrong with the horse I traded to the plaintiff. I told him I didn't know and that it looked like wire scratches but that there couldn't possibly be any fraud or disease spreading there, for "who," I told him, "would deliberately inflict wire scratches on a horse, even if you call it a disease?"

138

The judge, evidently, couldn't think of anyone off hand who would be so calloused as to do that. He wanted to know then what had become of the horse and mule and I told him that I had sold the horse for a hundred and twelve dollars and fifty cents, which was at least mathematically correct. I added that the horse was in good condition, also the mule, but that the iron-gray was over in the next county.

Well, the judge pondered the matter in that profound way that judges affect and delivered his decision just as solemnly, "I find that the defendant has proved that he isn't quilty as charged and I hereby acquit him."

The old Dutchman, glaring at the court and curious hangers-on, heaved himself out of the improvised court room, followed by his wife Frieda, a discouraged looking hired man, and the seedy lawyer he had engaged for no particular reason since it was a criminal prosecution.

The best part of the whole thing however was that he later bought his brown mule back for slightly less than seventy-five dollars. I was always good at figuring profits on horse trades but when I came to try and calculate the Dutchman's end of the deal it had me stumped. He probably never figured it out either, but if he ever tried he must have ended up slightly dizzy.

The Old Arsenic Treatment

The absence of the generally accepted system of police, lawyers, and courts in horse trading circles did not mean, however, that there was no justice. Horse traders took their lumps, nursed their wounds, and learned their lessons, but when they had the chance they also corrected any deals they had suffered that might have been particularly galling, and in such cases the justice was truly poetic, as described by Lew Croughan in this next tale.

One day in the early '90's I was passing along a country road in the eastern part of Dodge County [Nebraska] when ahead of me loomed up one of the most ramshackle farm buildings I had ever laid eyes on. The barn, a great, gaunt, unpainted building, had partly fallen in and leaned at such an awkward angle that I wondered why it hadn't collapsed long before. Several other rickety buildings and a desolate looking house were scattered about in a happy-go-lucky arrangement.

Everything else around the farmyard was in complete accord with the buildings and general disorder, such as a broken-down wagon, several empty barrels, and some rusty farm machinery. By the barn stood a tottering, shaggy gray horse, whose bones stuck out of his body like lattice work.

That horse's thinness fascinated me so much that in order to get a better view of him I turned my rig into a littered driveway and rolled up in the yard between the house and the tumble-down barn. The horse didn't take the trouble to raise his head, but the commotion of my arrival aroused some interest in the house. A backdoor opened and a tall, lanky man, almost as skinny as the horse, peered out to see what was going on. When he saw my outfit he turned to talk to someone inside for a minute, then he stepped out on a broken porch and came toward the wagon with a shuffling stride, that only the very lazy or physically weak fall into.

The man was about six feet tall but so gaunt and emaciated that he gave the illusion of having a much greater height. "Sure a sorry, scraggy looking outfit," I thought to myself as he approached my wagon with a question-mark expression on his face.

"Howdy, my friend," I greeted him. His hollow, lack-luster eyes fixed themselves upon me before he replied.

"Tolerable, tolerable, stranger. You aimin' to hit in round hereabouts?" He probably thought I was a new settler moving into the community, so I told him I might if it looked all right.

"But," I added motioning toward his skinny nag, "see you got a ganted horse there and just stopped to see him a bit closer. My name's Croughan, what's yours, friend?"

140

Now, a traveling horse trader doesn't waste much time fooling with names, especially his own, but I was curious to learn something about such a run-down looking layout.

"Mine's Pike," he volunteered. "Fortney Pike, and I hails from Missouri." I might have known that; the place was a typical Missouri set-up.

Then I got to visiting with him. It seems that he had come to Nebraska about ten years before with some money an aunt had left him and picked out that place, which must have reminded him of home. He was probably homesick anyway.

He looked over my string, then remarked that he "didn't never have no luck with hosses," that "mules was the only thing." But, it turned out, he didn't have a mule on the place. Just a small string of mangy horses. Out of curiousity I asked him about the skinny horse, which hadn't moved out of its tracks since I had arrived at the place.

"Stranger," he said, "there's a funny howdy-do about that hoss." Here he paused and seemed lost in thought, then he suddenly brightened up and began eyeing me in a serious manner before he continued. "Stranger, how would you like a good drenchin' of 'cawn'?"

Now this strange dialect might have had some folks guessing as to what he was driving at, but not me. I understood the invitation to have a snort of liquor in any man's language. Somewhat surprised at the invitation but entirely willing to accept it I heartily agreed that it would be about as fine as anything I could think of.

He shuffled over to a wooden rain barrel by a corner of the house where he hauled out a two-gallon stone jug, which was dripping with moisture as he brought it over to the wagon. I climbed down off the wagon seat in jig time when he extended the jug to me with the remark, "Here's my best cawn. You-all take a big swig." Maybe you've already guessed that no one has had to hold me while they poured liquor down my hatch. When drinking out of a big jug you can take on a good load without knowing it, and I am no exception.

The stuff wasn't bad at all. In fact it was as smooth as maple syrup with the power of carbolic acid. I was used to taking my whisky straight, so I didn't even come up for air until I had guzzled about a pint of the "red eye." He watched me, sort of contented like and not in the least perturbed. After I was through drinking he took a good jolt before returning the jug to the barrel.

"That's good liquor," I told him. "Does it keep better in water?"

"I don't reckon it helps much," he answered slow-like, "but there's a few snoopy folks round hereabouts who air too infernal lazy to fix a mess of cawn themselves and come traipsin' over to hog mine down. So I jes' keep it hid away from them. Why, them varmints'll just tramp into a feller's house lookin' for cawn."

The "cawn" began to get in its good work on me and I was becoming more cheerful every minute. "Tell me about that skin-and-bones horse you got there, friend," I said. I was curious to know a little more about the animal, seeing he had remarked just before he dug up that liquor, "There's a funny howdy-do about that hoss." He must have downed a pretty good snort of that "cawn" himself, for he was feeling pretty jovial by this time. His gaunt face lighted up at my mention of the horse.

I'll tell the story as Pike told it to me. It seems that he had a lame mule around the place so took a notion to get a horse in its place. The mule wasn't much of an animal evidently but he did have some meat on him. A trading outfit came along at this time. It consisted of a covered wagon and three or four snides of horses, a man, his slatternly woman, and a mess of kids. Pike said they hailed from Missouri, but I am not so sure about that, considering the trick he worked on Pike. Anyway, it would be a natural thing for a clever trader to work the "old home state" gag when he found out where Pike hailed from.

The self-styled Missourian claimed he was no horse trader, just an emigrant "a-comin' to Newbraskee." He had Pike's skin-and-bones horse trailing loose behind his outfit. One horse can be trusted to follow without a hitch, but not two or more. Pike said the "funny howdy-do" part of the deal was that the skinny horse looked plump and even a little frisky and,

142

mind you, only two weeks had elapsed since the trade. After the trade the stranger was on his way with Pike's mule, five dollars in cash, and a gallon of rain-barrel "cawn."

"But," Pike told me, "I never set eyes on sech a critter as that hoss turned out to be. The feller hadn't gotten out of seein' distance till my new hoss let out a couple of grunts and stumbled over to the barn and propped himself agin it. He started to 'gant up' then. After a few days he naturally caved in like you see 'im now. The danged critter won't eat nuthin, and he caint hardly stand now. He sure ain't worth a cuss for nuthin'. My ol' mule could work enough to make his salt."

At this point Pike seemed to feel the need of a little more uplift, so he shuffled unsteadily to the rain barrel where he finished out his jug again. Uncorking it he downed a stiff swig of the stuff. I thought he was going to put it back in the water, when he slapped the cork back in, but instead he jerked his head for me to come over. After another good pull at the jug I felt as if I could take over the world and get some cash boot along with it.

Then he plopped the jug back in the rain barrel and coughed a little nervously. "Wal," he asked a little thickly, "What in the shades of perdition is wrong with that there critter?"

Before answering Pike's question I walked on to take a close look at the scarecrow snide. My first observation was that the horse must have been thirty years old. His teeth were worn, the "cups" were gone, and the gums were shrunk away so's you could look right through his mouth. He was just an old wornout horse. That was obvious. What bothered me was Pike's story about the horse being plump and fleshed up a few weeks before. There is a way to bloat up a horse's carcass to make him look in better flesh, and I began to wonder if the Missourian hadn't worked it on Pike. You take a little arsenic, what you can raise on the point of a knife, and put it on the tonsils or the tongue. This poison immediately makes the horse pick up in looks and action. After continuing this treatment a few days you'll swear the animal is fattening up. But it isn't genuine; he's just bloated with water and if you rub your hand

143

over his sides you will find that they feel like a hot water bottle that has been filled with water. If you press in on the hide it will leave a dent. A horse treated with arsenic perks up and eats, his eyes shine like diamonds in a nigger's heel, and generally he can stay on his feet and give a good imitation of an animal with a lot of action. I took a look at the snide's tongue and, sure enough, the tongue was pitted around the tonsils, like arsenic is apt to do.

Pike looked on, his sunken eyes a little bleary, while I inspected the snide. When I was through he said with a voice thick from too much whisky, "Shtranger, a-wash matter of that air critter?"

"Well," I told him, "it's just an old worn-out pelter ready for the glue factory."

Pike thought that over for a minute and then said, "You-all kin have him, but ah cain't figure whash ails the hoss now. He sure was fatted up t'other day."

If it hadn't been for that rain barrel "cawn" I probably wouldn't have thought of doing what I did, but at tHe moment nothing looked impossible. It wound up by my taking the skinny snide as a gift. The bargain was sealed with another good pull at the jug.

I got the old snag tied to the back end of the wagon and started on my way, hoping the snide would stay on his pins, because I doubted even twisting its tail would get him up once he was down. The rain-barrel whisky was by now getting in some good work, but it only bothered me by making me too optimistic. My last glimpse of Pike showed him bending over the rain barrel again. I wondered if he had decided to make a day of it, and celebrate his good luck of getting shut of his worthless plug.

My only reason for taking the snag was because of a hazy idea of charging him up with arsenic and hanging him onto someone with more horses than brains. I was also curious to find out how he would react to this powerful drug. Off hand I'd say he was beyond even temporary redemption.

The old pelter managed to keep on his feet until I came to a town with a drugstore, where I bought arsenic for my exper-

144

iment. The druggist was an inquisitive old cuss that wanted to know my business, including what I was going to do with the arsenic. I joshed him by answering it was for a rich uncle who had named me in his will.

He laughed a little uneasily, "Ha ha! That's a good joke." Then I told him it was for a stifled horse and since he didn't know what a stifled horse was, he let the matter drop.

Well, sir, you'd be surprised how that old bag of bones perked up when I started the arsenic treatment. He seemed to like it and I wondered if the stuff didn't make him feel good as well as look better. It was astounding how that horse reacted. He just seemed to put on flesh before your eyes and began shying around like a young colt. His ribs ceased pertruding through the skin and his joints smoothed out. Even his shrunken eyes came up in their sockets and began to look normal. I couldn't help but wonder how a little arsenic would affect the old pelter's former owner, Pike, who was as skin-poor as the horse had been.

Of course the snide's fleshy look was just liquid under the hide and when you rubbed him he had a squashy feeling. As I continued the treatment he began looking better every day. He was eating too, though his teeth weren't much good.

It's funny how I got rid of that old plug. An enormously big man who was driving a team of shaggy, big-boned plow horses hitched to a spring wagon came along one evening when I was preparing to camp for the night. He pulled up with a loud "Whoa!" as he looked me over insolently.

"So ho," he blared out, "so if it ain't the old travelin' horse trader." He was, I could see, a smart aleck but then they were no rarity in those days. "I'll give you fifty dollars for your whole damned outfit," he sarcastically added.

"You mean you'll give fifty dollars a head, don't you, friend? They're worth a hundred."

He guffawed at that but didn't make any move of leaving. The old bone bag was looking pretty slick, being well primed with arsenic, so the big-mouthed geek got to looking at him. Of course you can't make a young horse out of an old one, but fleshing them up works wonders in that same direction.

145

Well, that big smart aleck hung around until I proposed a trade. "Nope," he says, "no trade, but I got ten dollars here for my pick of one of your crow baits."

"No," answered, "but I'll tell you what I will do." I pointed at the old snag and said, "You can have this good old family horse for twenty-five dollars."

He laughed and slapped his knee at my proposal. "Gosh, that's a good 'un all right, all rightie," he boomed at me, looking like he was about to be doubled up with mirth.

"Oh well, friend, I wouldn't want to sell him anyway. Just wanted to be a good sport," I told him.

I didn't have the least idea he had any intention of doing business, so you can imagine my satisfaction when he bounced out of his spring wagon to have a closer look at the bone-bag horse. He even untied him and led him around. My trader's instinct told me that for some fool reason the smart aleck was interested in the old pelter. He didn't waste any time neither in fishing out some bills from his pocket.

"Here," he said, "take fifteen dollars and I'll take this plug off your hands." I pretended to draw back at his offer but took care to grab the fifteen dollars.

After he had tied the old pelter to his own wagon, he crawled back up on the seat, his weight causing the front end of his rig to settle about a foot on the springs. He clucked to his plow team. As they moved off, he turned and shouted, "Thanks, stranger. This is the kind of a plug I want my ol' woman to drive. He ain't so apt to run away or get skeared and dump the buggy over."

I sure could agree with him on that one. It must have been my calling the snag a "family horse" that aroused the old boy's interest. I would have liked to have been around when the snag had used up the arsenic that was in his system and reverted back to his normal self. The smart aleck, when this occurred, must have thought I had the horse hypnotized.

Anyway, he had it coming for being a smart aleck.

All the Ribs on One Side

The next story, about a horse with all of his ribs on one side, as unlikely as that might seem, is a perfect example of the inherent contradictions that existed with the world of horse traders. Normally, a horse with such a massive defect would have been avoided at all costs, and any owner would have gone to any extent to disguise the fault. But of course this mistake of nature was far too obvious and total to permit disguise. So, according to all rules of logic, this worthless creature should have been shot or sold to a glue factory, right?

Wrong! The smart trader seizes the opportunity, and turns it to his very substantial financial advantage.

The most acute problem with this story is that Lew Croughan may have been pulling a fast one on Harold J. Moss and thus on us. Is there really such a thing as a horse (yet two!) with its ribs all on one side? All livestock experts I have discussed the matter with have responded with an incredulous "Absolutely not!" On the other hand there was the afterthought of one such expert: "Of course since calves are sometimes born with two heads, I suppose anything is possible." True or not, it is a good story!

One day, as I was passing a farm near Tekamah [Nebraska], I saw the queerest looking horse I had ever laid eyes on. Its back was high-arched and lop-sided. I stopped to make a closer inspection of what looked like a freak to me.

The farmer happened to be around and obligingly offered to bring the horse out of the feed yard. I thought he was stringing me when he said the horse had a double row of ribs on one side and none on the other. But sure enough, that's the way he was built. His ribs were all on the right side. The fellow said he could work in harness but couldn't be ridden. I thought the farmer was looking for a trade, so I began wondering what I might do with the horse if I traded.

147

We talked a while, and then the fellow suddenly asked me if I wanted to take the horse along. "What do you want for him?" I asked, sounding him out on a trade.

"Nothing," he answered. "I don't want to trade. But if you want him take him along."

I figured the horse would be a "white elephant" to me, but I was curious to see what I could do with him. Then the farmer told me he knew where I could get a mate to the freak, only this other horse had all his ribs on the left side, but had the same arched back. It seems, he told me, that both freaks were born of the same mare, who evidently specialized in freak, lop-sided colts. When he told me where the other horse could be found I decided to take his one-sided animal. But, although he tried to give him to me, I handed him two dollars and a half. He threw in a rope halter. I knew if I could get the other horse I would be able to cash in on a matched team of freaks. I noticed, as I drove out of the farmer's yard, that the freak horse led good and seemed tough enough to stand travel.

I now altered my course slightly and headed for the place where the other horse was supposed to be. It was on the far side of the next township but the directions the fellow had given were easy to follow. That night I approached what looked to be the place. After thinking it over, I decided to camp and wait until morning before I tackled the farmer.

The next morning I hid my freak horse in a small draw before I drove over to see the farmer who was supposed to have the mate to my freak. He eyed me suspiciously from his barn where he was rigging up a block and tackle. Ignoring his sullen mood I hailed him with a cheery, "Morning, friend. Any mules hereabouts that I could deal for?" I knew better than to ask him about freak horses, because if he knew that I was interested, he would hike up his price, like all farmers did if they had half a chance.

His only reply was a grunt or a shake with his head, but I noted a gleam of speculation in his small, button-like eyes. He was a hard pill to handle, all right, but I kept at him.

"I could use a horse or two, though I don't want anything extra good," I continued. His only reply was to pluck a straw

148

from the ground, put it in his mouth, and thoughtfully chew on it. After an awkward silence he gave a little cough, and then in a drawling voice said, "Wal, now stranger, I don't set much store by you hoss traders. You're always out to skin us farm folks."

I hastened to reassure him that nothing could be further from my thoughts. Besides, I was just asking for a little information. I couldn't see into his barn but it was a pretty big one, so I figured he would have a lot of horses around.

He reluctantly came over to the wagon to have a look at my string. "You sure got an ornery looking parcel of plugs, stranger," he drawled. This remark was better than I had expected, because when a man starts running down your trading stock it's usually a sign that he's interested in a trade.

"Well, friend, I've got plenty of cash that wouldn't look so ornery to you." This remark caused him to warm up. I noticed a spark of interest in his eye at the mention of cash.

I then talked him into letting me see his horses, and even I was surprised when I saw his stable. He must have had fifteen head in there, including a span of mules and four big Norman work horses. But I saw no sign of the freak horse, and I began to think I had either come to the wrong place or else he didn't have a freak after all. I asked if his name was Gomer and he 'lowed as it was, so that checked all right, that being the name the other fellow had given me.

Then I saw a box stall at the far end of the building that was boarded up so high I couldn't see into it. What aroused my curiosity was that in addition to being latched, the door was also locked with a padlock. I tried to look over the boarded wall, through the bars, but found I couldn't see anything without hoisting myself up. And I couldn't do that because the farmer kept an uneasy eye on me. The stall was tightly boxed, but I located a small crack on the front side. Just then somebody called from the house, causing the farmer to go to the barn door. While his back was turned I bent down and peeked through the crack.

What I saw gave me a thrill, for there stood the other freak horse, and his double ribs were arranged opposite of the
149

one I had cached out in the draw. As near as I could make out he was a white and pink spotted brown, a good color combination for a show horse, which is what I intended selling them for. The two horses, on account of their freakish rib growth, would be a sensation in any circus sideshow.

Gomer came back before I had finished looking through the crack, so he must have seen what I was doing. I thought it time to sound him out, so acting a little apologetic, just to make it look good, I told him I thought he had a stallion in the box and I was always interested in them. He looked at me for a full half minute before he replied in his whiney voice, "Mebbe you're one of those here pesky folks that's been goin' around snoopin' to see if we're bein' ornery to animals. That there's why I got that hoss in the box, dang their souls!" Then he unlocked the door to the box and let out the horse.

He told me that he'd bought the lop-sided freak from a stranger "over to Adsits Corners," wherever that might be. He just bought it, he said, "cause the fellow offered it cheap. A few days before I had seen the horse a feller had come to Adsits Corners offering five hundred dollars for a freak horse wanted by a circus." It seems that a few days later when Gomer was over to Adsits Corners again a trader came along with the freak horse that the other man had offered five hundred dollars for.

Gomer's suspicion and reticence towards me quickly evaporated as he warmed up on the subject, which had probably been bothering him more than anyone surmised. As his enthusiasm mounted, his drawl and whine subsided and he talked faster and with more emphasis and gestures.

"The feller," Gomer said, "who was a-hankerin' to buy a freak hoss for five hundred dollars had tole me he would be back to Adsits Corners the coming Tuesday when mebbe I could hep 'im find that funny hoss, which he had heard was out in these parts. So when this feller came long leading this lop-sided critter I jes up and dickered for 'im, seein's that that other feller wanted him so bad."

I was now curious to know what Gomer paid for the horse, so put out a feeler. He hesitated a little, but what he told me

150

made me wonder what he would call "dear," if the price he paid was "cheap." He had paid a hundred and fifty dollars for that soft-sided horse. Now I began to get the picture. Those two rascals were in cahoots and had fixed up a deal on Gomer. What they had used was an old sucker trick, but one that was always good.

"How come," I asked him, "you have the horse now when you could have turned him to the circus agent for five hundred dollars?"

Gomer plucked another straw and began chewing it in an agitated manner, then he shook a work-hardened finger at me as he shouted, "That danged coyote never come back, so now I have this hoss on my hands and he ain't worth a stick of stove wood to me!"

The whole thing was funny all right. And Gomer's earlier remark concerning "pesky folks who come snoopin' around to see if we're ornery to animals" caused me to suspect there was more to Gomer's story than he had already told.

After acquiring the freak horse Gomer had hitched it to the back of a cart and driven over to Adsits Corners (which seemed to be his private hangout) with the hope of meeting the man who had offered five hundred dollars for the horse. But, instead of meeting that chap, he ran afoul of a stern-looking individual, a stranger in these parts, who had the gall, Gomer said, "to stick his oar in, and threaten to have me arrested for being ornery to dumb animals. Drivin' a poor crippled hoss that had ought to be out resting in some pasture," was the way the fellow had said it. The man, Gomer said, "had some kind of a constable's badge hitched to his galluses and was a wearin' a big, black hat."

Gomer, knowing nothing about any such business as cruelty to animals, became so worried after hearing these accusations that he was at a loss as how to proceed with the stranger, who continued glaring accusingly at him. "A passel of nosey loafers gathered about," Gomer continued, "and that plagued me, having 'em gawking and laughing."

The crowd was no doubt more interested in the freak horse than in what the stranger said, but the whole setup was exciting enough, with what seemed to be a representative of the law present.

Gomer must have been sufficiently impressed because he said he asked the officious stranger if it would be all right if he drove the horse home. The stranger, according to Gomer, then put on another act, demanding five dollars for the issuance of a permit. At this point Gomer recovered some of his gumption and told the fellow to go plum to hell and that he would rather sell him the horse for five dollars.

Added Gomer, "And danged if that feller didn't up and say he'd take 'im for five. That remark made me mad and I told him he could go hang. Then he said he'd give me ten dollars for him and afore I got goin' he had 'hepped' it up to twenty-five dollars with the remark that if I didn't take that, he'd have to arrest me and take the hoss anyhow. I had told him to go ahead when 'Hod' Fisher, the blacksmith, came up wearin' his leather apron. 'Just let the scaliwag try it,' he roared, 'and I'll take him down to the shop and bend him around the anvil.'"

Well, Gomer told me he climbed back into his cart and the stranger edged out of the crowd and wasn't seen when Gomer and his freak horse departed on their way homeward.

I knew now that the gang Gomer had been dealing with were trying to put a three-way deal on him, expecting to get the freak back for little or nothing by staging the old cruelty-to-animals gag. This outfit, evidently, valued the freak pretty high and for the present they were using him as bait for the suckers.

Gomer was now my friend and asked me to stay for dinner. I didn't say anything about buying his freak until we got up from the table when I said, "I don't suppose that horse is much good to anyone anyway. You will have him on your hands to feed for a long spell, besides giving him the best stall in your barn."

He studied me with his funny button eyes for a while and then said, "I calculate to keep him out of sight so them danged nosey critters won't come a-pesterin' me none about bein' ornery to him."

Gomer was taking the cruelty-to-dumb-animals gag more seriously than I had thought. Well, I was now on the good side of the old boy, so along in the middle of the afternoon we wandered out to the barn to have another look at the freak horse. In order to better show me the curious malformed "barrel" of the horse he brought him out of the stall. I wondered at the gentleness of the unfortunate animal until I discovered his ribless side was tender, thus discouraging any violent action.

Gomer asked me what I thought about the horse. I told him chances were that he'd have to shoot the poor beast eventually since he couldn't dispose of him. "But," I added, "I know a rich old man down in my territory who makes a hobby of collecting disabled horses and giving them a home and a well-earned rest." Of course that was stretching the truth considerably but I had to think of something that would lead up to my proposition of taking the horse off of Gomer's hands.

"It's a shame to have to kill the poor beast. He's such a likable horse," I added.

Some of Gomer's enthusiasm had dropped away by this time, but he still clung to the idea that maybe that "circus feller" would come along with five hundred dollars for the freak horse. However, he didn't have too much hope, so after a little talking he sold me the horse for twenty-five dollars.

I was now in a hurry to get away, since the horse's freak mate was still staked out in the gully, so I bid Gomer good-bye and pulled out, leading the pathetic high-backed equine. I never expected to see his owner again. After retrieving the horse in the gully I set out in the general direction of my base, leading the two freaks behind my covered wagon. It must have been a strange looking procession to the citizenry along the way.

I could have followed the road which led by Gomer's house and saved a mile or so, but decided to avoid any chance of meeting with him, since the shock of seeing two freaks where but one existed before might be a little too much for the old boy. So I headed down a seldom used crossroad which was just

153

a grassy trail and figured he would have to have field glasses to make me out at that distance.

But I didn't know that Gomer's land extended clear down to that road. As I jogged along, well out of sight of the buildings, I suddenly saw a horseman on a chestnut sorrel top a ridge on the prairie. He was riding in my general direction, although he evidently wasn't particularly heading towards me. I wasn't concerned much until the rider angled towards my outfit. Then I became disturbed because it was Gomer. Of course when he recognized my outfit he headed over to me.

It was funny to see the blank, incredulous look on Gomer's moon face when he saw the two freaks. He stared at them, then passed his hand across his face, as if attempting to brush aside a bad vision, for what he saw had to be unreal. I grinned a little sheepishly and give him the "horse trader's salute," which is a sweeping gesture that always seems to include the earth and all that's on it.

"Danged if I ain't seein' double," he shouted. "Where in tarnation hell did you fetch up with that other critter?"

My deal with him had been made so I could afford to tell him the truth. He just sat there on his horse sort of like he was in a trance. He just gawked as I drove away. Not a word did he utter. About forty rods on down the trail I turned and looked back. Gomer was riding slowly toward home, much like a man who had just awakened from a bad dream.

I never saw him again but I often thought about the bizarre chain of circumstances which led up to his paying a hundred and fifty dollars for a freak horse and then selling it for twenty-five dollars.

What took place later made me wonder if the "circus man" in Gomer's story and his offer of five-hundred dollars for the horse might not have been genuine after all. I sold that pair of soft-sided, high-backed horses to a circus for two thousand two hundred and fifty dollars.

Corking a Pelter

A former salesman for a particularly notorious used car dealer in Lincoln tells me that the older cars, the dogs, are parked out close to the very busy street in the front of the lot because there the traffic noise will cover up the sounds of mechanical carnage in ruined engines and transmissions. This very same routine was done with bad-winded horses; they would be sold near a cattle pen, on a busy town corner, by a large river, or beside a running threshing machine to cover up the sounds of their afflictions. Putting sawdust or oatmeal in the transmission and thick oil in the engine of a car to make it seem tighter is not very different from plugging the nostrils of a bull windy, as in the following story which Harold J. Moss collected from E. L. Smach of Lincoln, Nebraska, on 24 and 25 July 1940.

In the days of many horses and few autos my brother-in-law dabbled in horse swappin' considerable and got a bad skinnin' in a trade with a windy farmer named Colbert up Ulysses [Nebraska] way. He had it in for old Colbert and schemed to get even somehow. In lookin' over a trader's stock one day he found just what he was lookin' for—a wind-broken nag that looked pretty good but wasn't. An old horseman had told him if he would take a wind-broke horse and shove a cork way up each nostril that the horse would breathe through his mouth and not make that ungodly wailing sound that always gives them away. The trader admitted the horse was wind-broke, there being little use to deny it as the horse played a tune with his breathin' apparatus every few minutes. A deal was made and for two dollars my brother-in-law had the horse.

He knew Colbert would be down in a day or two, as he had some interests around Syracuse including a farm. Well, Colbert showed up and he had a good-lookin' team, but he also kept some pretty fair horses at his place down there. It was no trouble for my brother-in-law to get him interested in a trade,

155

for Colbert had come out so golden on the last one that he looked on him as a kind of a sucker.

Colbert drove over, leading a rather rangy lookin', dark brown horse, a little raw-boned but not bad. Ed—that's my brother-in-law—had his old wind-broke pelter all fixed up for the occasion. He had a cork poked away up each nostril, each cork having a bit of string attached to it so that the corks could be removed without too much fuss. Ed's horse didn't size up bad if only he wouldn't start whistling and wailing through his nose.

But the corks did the trick and not a peep came out of him while Colbert was lookin' him over. They traded and Colbert took his new horse, corks and all, back to his place.

That night Ed slipped over and succeeded in getting those corks out without being seen. As he left he could hear the nightmarish sounds the wind-broke pelter let go with, making up for lost time when he found his nostrils open once more. Colbert swore plenty next morning when he discovered the condition of his horse and wondered why it hadn't shown up when he was makin' the trade. For a time nothing was said, but the story was too good to keep and it got around.

Ed's horse turned out to be fairly sound and he sold him outright for forty dollars some time later. Colbert stayed mad for several weeks and then forgot about the whole thing.

The Bay With One Flaw

Although it might surprise twentieth-century readers, blindness was not so serious an affliction, especially in draught animals that could be taught to perform flawlessly to the signals of the reins—sometimes with such deceptive precision that a buyer could be lured into a trade, never questioning the horses' eyes because of their deftness in driving.

Another tale from the same trader's experience—

There was a man named Imen, a rather dignified and efficient figure, cowhide boots, bushy whiskers, and tall hat, and he made a fool horse trader even though he was supposed to be an expert horseman. This happened about the turn of the century down at Syracuse, Nebraska.

This feller Imen had a dandy team, sound as a dollar and wonderful pullers. They was nigh perfect in every way except they wasn't a matched team. One was a bay and the other a gray. Much as Imen liked that team, their clashing colors bothered him.

One day he drove the team to Syracuse to get some repairs and started home about "cow time" with the sun gettin' low in the west. Just east of town he met up with a horse trader who appeared to be journeying west but who could have been laying low for Imen. This tradin' feller had a dandy lookin' horse which just about matched Imen's team in size, color, and general appearance.

He hailed Imen and started talking trade, spreadin' it on thick about what a fine, sound horse he had, which was also a perfect match for Imen's bay. Imen, of course, could see that for himself and he couldn't help bein' a little interested.

The trader led his bay out and invited Imen to look it over. Imen was impressed and gave that horse a rigid examination. He looked at its teeth, felt over every inch of its legs and body, threw dust in its nostrils, walked it backward to see if it might be stiff in the legs, and gouged its belly with a stick to determine if it might be wind-broke. In fact, he did about everything to test that horse out, even to a fast trot down the road.

Nothing happened. The horse responded nobly to every test. But Imen, smart horseman that he was, failed to do one thing. That was to examine the horse's eyes.

They fooled around quite a while and finally just at dusk completed the trade. The timing of the whole thing was most excellent for the horse trader. For a blind horse is apt to perform better at night than in the broad daylight, and his blindness is less noticeable.

157

Well, old Imen hitched in his new bay and drove off. The trader did the same, but in the opposite direction.

Imen got home a little late and unhitched. He still didn't notice anything wrong but when he led his new horse into its stall, that "critter" tried to walk right through the manger. His suspicions aroused, Imen led the horse out into the yard and turning its head toward the moon he stared at its eyes. No light reflected from them. The horse was blind as an owl in sunlight.

Imen, who prided himself on his horses and his ability to judge one, woefully reflected on the whole matter and felt like kickin' himself around the hog house. Although he kept the thing to himself as long as possible, it was only natural that his new horse came in for lots of attention, which resulted in the affair becoming common knowledge and laying him open to a lot of humiliating wise cracks.

The Stump Sucker

From the high Plains of Texas to the prairie Plains of the Dakotas they were called stump suckers and in the East they were called cribbers. Everywhere they were trouble and gave more ammunition to nagging wives than any other creature that walked the earth before the pickup truck. The horse showed no flaws whatever until the original owner was well out of sight, and then the effects were indeed spectacular, as the following tale—a classic of its sort—shows.

The story was collected from Grant Dehart of Lincoln, Nebraska, in 1940 by an unidentified fieldworker. It was previously published in my Treasury of Nebraska Pioneer Folklore.

A neighboring horse trader who lived ten miles from our place pulled into the yard one morning, driving what seemed to be a fair to middling good work team. The off horse, however, aroused my suspicions although he was a big-boned gray who was as sleek and well fleshed as a ripened watermelon. In fact, he was too sleek. If he had acted sick I would have thought he was bloated. But some horses look that way for no particular reason. Father, of course, was circling around him in his best professional manner, but then he did that to every horse he saw. Anyway, Swapper apparently wasn't bent on a trade. His coming looked like a sociable drop-in that so many folks were in the habit of doing in those days. Besides, he said he was on his way on an important errand elsewhere.

But father, who was becoming interested in the gray, didn't listen to Swapper's talk about leaving. There was something about the gray that had captured his eye. I suppose it was his sleek appearance—the same sleek appearance that had aroused my suspicions.

So, knowing of father's interest, I wasn't surprised when he went into the barn and brought out an eight-year-old bay mare he had traded for a few months before. She was a good piece of horseflesh except for her bad habit of riding the singletree [letting the other horse do all the pulling] when doing team work.

Swapper, as soon as father began showing her off, forgot all about the hurry he had said he was in. Instead he sat down and slowly filled his pipe with corncake.

"I tell you, Dehart," said Swapper, now leisurely puffing away on his briar, "I'm not hankering to part with Gray Bill. He's too good a hoss. But, as a personal favor, I might be willing to trade for your mare if you will throw in a little boot—say $15."

This offer started father and Swapper off into a typical horsetrader's argument, with Swapper trying to keep his original price where he had placed it and father attempting to cut it down to what he regarded as a more reasonable figure.

They finally struck a compromise of $7.50 and it looked like a trade. I noticed that father was now in such a hurry to finish the deal he neglected to ask some of the usual trader's questions about hidden defects. His only one was when he asked, "Your gray ain't wind-broke, is he?"

159

Swapper, in an insulted tone, answered, "Look here, De-hart, you'll find that hoss has more wind than any hoss you ever had."

Well, this answer settled the deal. They made the swap. Our bay was harnessed and hitched in jig time. Father led Gray Bill off to the side while Swapper got into his buggy, gathered up the lines and then, after mumbling something about being in a hurry, went away rather suddenlike. His actions still seemed queer to me, but I didn't say anything.

Father, after Swapper had left, took Gray Bill into the barn and tied him in a stall that had a straight pole running across. It was now eleven-thirty. The horse trade had taken most of the morning, so I didn't see how Swapper could have been in a hurry after spending so much time with us. Father, however, thought he had done a good morning's work; but I reserved my conclusions. Gray Bill still seemed too perfect. He was so sleek that he looked more like a shiny, over-sized toy horse than the real thing.

About half an hour later we all sat down to dinner, but only had time to pass the food around before an infernal racket started in the barn. It sounded like a dozen bellows and a hundred frogs all blowing and croaking in unison. It went "ooph ker chug, ooph ker chug," and then for variety reversed itself to "chug ker ooph, chug ker ooph." Hell had certainly broken loose in the barn.

Ma was the first to jump up. She yelled, "Pa, that's your new horse! You and your smart horse swapping has gotten us a stump sucker!"

Sure enough, when we got to the barn we found Gray Bill with his jaws clamped on the pole that ran across the manger, making the most unearthly noises I have ever heard. He was sucking wind like a cow pulling her foot out of the mud.

It was a sight to see and I couldn't help but laugh. "Yep, you've got a wind sucker there for fair."

Father was raving mad. "That skunk, Swapper, knew about this."

"Well, didn't he tell you Gray Bill had more wind than any horse around here?" I asked.

160

The horse was blowed up like a balloon and still going strong. I thought he'd bust, but he didn't. That was why he looked so fat and sleek when Swapper drove him in. The old rascal had stopped the horse at a post and let him suck wind just before he came to our house.

We thought we could bring him out of his wind-sucking habit by keeping him away from wooden fences or poles, but that was a difficult thing to do. Then too, he wouldn't eat much, so as soon as his "wind pressure" went down he looked like a walking skeleton. I doubt if he ate more than half a dozen mouthfuls of hay a day—just enough to keep from falling over.

The first thing father did the next Sunday morning was to drive over to Swapper's place with the stump sucker. To his surprise Swapper was unusually lenient for being a horse trader. He offered to exchange the bay mare for Gray Bill provided he could keep the $7.50. Father was glad to get out of the deal this easy.

Later we learned that Swapper had traded his stump sucker to nearly every newcomer in the county. Swapper always got him back, keeping, of course, the money that had been involved in the transactions.

A Genuine Freak

Of course horse trading was a game of wits and could get into your blood. It is my conviction that those most perfidious instincts in a man that lead him down the crooked paths of trading are brought to the surface by the even darker nature of the horse. I offer the following story by way of evidence that not just in trading but wherever men and horses come together there is good reason to tread with a cautious step. Harold J. Moss collected the material from Lew Croughan of Lincoln at an unspecified date.

[Croughan describes a wandering carnival that passed through northern Nebraska in the early 1900s.]

It wasn't much of a show but had the usual line of cheap gambling games, clip joints, high pitch artists and trick side shows with their lurid painted fronts and leather-lunged spielers. Being, of course, "horse conscious" one of the side shows sort of fascinated me. Though I figured it was a fake of some kind. It seemed to be getting a good play too—gaping crowds in front and a line of the local rubes pushing their way into the dirty canvas-shrouded interior. Grinning a little sheepishly, those who had already viewed the wonders within were exiting from another opening in the canvas wall. The spieler was doing a good job of it, the sweat trickling down his face as he harangued the crowd in front, meantime intermittently slapping his cane against a gaudy painted canvas directly behind and above him.

"Good neighbors and horse lovers, see the result of nature's cruel trick against man's noblest friend. You'll shudder and shiver when you behold this poor animal, the pathetic victim of the world's strangest zoological slip-up. Anthropologists have viewed this extraordinary specimen and found themselves completely baffled. It's the only known case in the world of yesterday or today—it's the horse which has his tail where his head ought to be!"

Here he lowered his voice, "But dear people, if you or your little ones are subject to shock and fright and sensitive to the horrors of nature's ghastly mistake, I pray you, do not enter this place. Do not allow your eyes to rest upon this monstrous example of one of God's creatures which stands there now with one end where the other ought to be. A thin dime, the tenth part of a dollar, admits you, but be prepared to see a sight which I warrant you have never seen before. It's the horse turned end for end!"

A "shill" stepped up and bought a ticket and the crowd fell over themselves to follow. Evidently they all thought they could survive the shock which the spieler had mentioned.

Those who came out after seeing the show didn't have much to say. They just went on their way. I did hear one farmer tell another who hadn't as yet gone in that he sure ought to see that show. That's the human nature for you every time. You make a sucker out of anyone and he'll turn right around and steer somebody else into it.

Thinking it was just a freak horse but willing to pay a dime to find out I fell in with the rest of the saps and in we went. They had a regular horse stall set up inside, manger and all, and in the stall stood an old snide of a horse. His tail was where his head should have been all right, for his tail was tied to the manger and his head stuck out from the back of the stall.

Trading by Moonlight

The following story is one of the few of this collection that has been published before. It was originally collected from Grant Dehart and appeared in my Treasury of Nebraska Pioneer Folklore. *Dehart died on 15 November 1955, at the age of ninety-two.*

A few years after father's horse trade with Swapper I got a job in a water mill near Central City [Nebraska]. When working there I made a horse trade with Swapper for what looked like a fair saddle horse whose name was Baldy. This horse was a smooth, bald-faced bay whose only apparent fault was that he had ornery eyes. I thought I could handle him if he got nasty, so his mean expression didn't bother me. It looked like a good deal.

But it didn't require a long time to find out he was just as ornery as he looked. He behaved fine at first, was so gentle that he could have been a ladies' horse. But our honeymoon was soon over with. One evening, when I was leaving Central City after visiting friends, I found myself sitting on Main

Street in a puddle of water with a bunch of loafers whooping and laughing around me.

The horse, who I soon began to suspect was the devil himself, didn't run away. Instead he stood still and actually looked amused as I started to get up. I managed to ride him home that night without being thrown a second time, but only because I didn't let him take me by surprise.

The next morning I fixed up a bucking stick, which is a crotched stick that is fastened to the belly band and runs up to the bridle-bit rings. This arrangement kept him from getting his head down so he could buck.

I was now anxious to get rid of Old Baldy before everyone in the neighborhood caught on that he was a bucker. So, with this in mind, I rode him one night to a party given a few miles south of the mill, where I hoped to meet someone who would be interested in a trade. I took off the bucking stick when I got near the place and tied him at the pasture gate, which was located some distance from the house. This was done to keep too many people from seeing and asking questions about him. The less advertising you do with a bad horse you wish to sell, the better off you are.

Lem Troost, who was a newcomer to the neighborhood, showed up at the party a little later and we got to discussing this and that. Finally we got on the subject of horses.

Lem said, "I sure got a bang-up smooth four-year-old filly out there." That remark of Lem's got me interested, so I began bragging up the bald-faced bucking boy Swapper had pawned off on me. Pretty soon we wandered into the yard to compare horses.

There was a good moon, which made Baldy look sleek and racy. Even his eyes had a gentle look. Lem immediately fell in love with my horse and wanted to ride him; but I was scared he would get hurt, and at the same time I didn't want to say anything about Baldy's bad habit of bucking.

Finally I gave in to Lem's request; but before I let him mount, I wheeled Baldy around so he would start off in the opposite direction from where he was standing. I had found he wouldn't buck when I did this, if he wasn't ridden for too great

164

a distance. I also told Lem my horse was used to me but might resent a stranger riding him at night. This was a hint for him to be on his guard. Lem mounted while I held my breath for fear he would be thrown off. But nothing happened. Baldy behaved like an angel, which made Lem fall more in love with him than ever.

Lem, after his ride, took me to a side of the barn where his horse was hitched. She wasn't as big as Baldy but looked good. I rode her around the yard in order to get the feel of her. The only thing I regretted was that there were too many rigs around to put her through a fast pace, which is the best way to test a horse.

We traded even, without any boot. Lem seemed anxious to get away after we had exchanged the saddles on our new horses. I would have noticed this more and become suspicious if I hadn't been of the same mind. The party, which was still in progress, was forgotten by both of us.

Lem was the first to leave. I wondered what would happen to him on his way home if Baldy began bucking, but I didn't actually worry because Lem was a good rider who wouldn't get hurt *much* if Baldy decided to give him a spill.

After Lem had left I started for home on my filly, and was delighted. I put her into a trot and then a gallop. We were breezing along at a good clip, feeling extra good, when for what seemed no reason at all she stumbled and went down. At first I thought it was an accident, but a little later it happened again—twice in one mile. I got skinned up that time, so went easy the rest of the way. I knew now that Lem had put over about the same thing on me that I had on him.

The next morning I found out what was the trouble with my new horse, although it took another bad fall to do it. She had a crooked foot which worked all right at a slow trot but when she went into a gallop the foot turned in, causing her to hit it with her other foot. She went down every time she did it.

Lem found out about his side of the trade the next morning when Baldy pitched him into the road. He didn't hang on to Baldy long after that had happened. This time he traded for a one-eyed, old pelter who had the heaves. Lem and I laughed over the way we thought we had out-smarted each other. We figured we had broken even, so remained friends—only we didn't trade any more horses.

The Roan That Didn't Look So Good

The following tale was collected by Harold J. Moss on 24 July 1940, from Robert Milton Murphy, who was eighty-two at the time and had arrived in Nebraska in 1873. The story has the classic traits of a horse-trading tale. The trader skillfully assumes the role of the reluctant party to the trade; he warns the prospective customer about the real fault of the animal, but in such language that the meaning is veiled; and at the conclusion of the story the trader is not the least bit moved by the pitiful complaints of the dupe, who, after all, had it coming.

We had a young roan mare, good build, sound wind, a sort of middleweight class, which might do equally well as a driver, saddle, or work horse. She was a pretty sightly piece of horse flesh but had one bad defect: She was blind.

A young feller who lived northwest from us got the tradin' bug and after a few more or less ordinary trades around the neighborhood, he got to thinkin' he was pretty good. He knew that we had that mare, but he didn't know she was blind.

One day in the '80's he rode bareback over to our place on a horse that come as near to a blue color as I ever had seen. He would have passed well as a plow horse and seemed sound enough. Young Tibbets, that was his name, claimed he had driven a shrewd deal with an emigrant outfit, passing through, and got hold of the animal pretty slick like, so he said.

Now a blind horse such as our mare was not altogether useless and in open places with good footing could get around very well. But they weren't rated very high in trading circles.

166

Tibbets had taken a shine to our blind mare and proposed a trade. I didn't want to trade with him and told him so. Still he insisted and hung around and I finally brought out "Puss," which was the name of the blind mare.

She did very well, getting about in familiar surroundings. Tibbets wanted that mare. I told him, "Now, young feller, I ain't anxious to trade. In fact, I don't even want to. You'd better keep your blue plug. You don't want that mare."

I run the mare down and did what I could to discourage him. I said, "There she is. She's a little rough and isn't very good at anything, just a combination drivin' and work plug. And for a drivin' horse she don't look very good."

In fact, she didn't look at all, bein' blind as a bat.

"Well," he said, "I'm satisfied"—he hadn't looked at her eyes. "I'll trade you as is. You can't fool me on a horse."

His horse wasn't so much but could see, anyway. It's funny but many a middlin' good trader forgets to look at a horse's eyes for some reason or other, though anyone who owns a blind horse is pretty conscious of them.

We made the trade, and Tibbets rode the mare off toward his dad's place. I saw her stumble once but he didn't catch on and soon was out of sight. The next day he was back with the mare a-cussin' and tearin' his hair. He'd found out what was wrong with his horse.

Says he, "The trade's off. This nag is blind as a bat. I want my plug back! It's a hell of a thing, puttin' off a blind mare on me!"

"Why," I says, "didn't you tell me that no one could fool you on a horse, you was that smart? Anyway, you traded as is, when I didn't even want to trade. Your old man's well fixed and I guess you can stand a little experience anyway. I ain't goin' to take that mare back. You recall that I told you she didn't look very good."

Croughan Goes to Court

*Sometimes the law could not be kept out of a trade. Sometimes
a newcomer to the business would take offense at an arrangement and would run to the sheriff. Sometimes even a seasoned
trader would find exception to a bargain that after the fact took
on new dimensions. So horse traders did occasionally find their
way into the unaccustomed environment of the court room. But
judges are usually horse traders themselves—in the court room
if not at the sale barn—and the frontier judge might often
recognize the sanctity of the as-is trade and advise the accuser
to accept the trade, uneven as it might seem, as a valuable
lesson in trading.*

*The Federal Writers Project files state that this narrative
was collected from Lew Croughan, but there is no further
information; it was, however, probably recorded by Harold J.
Moss.*

A horse trader on the road would often find himself in some
queer situations. It's funny the way people were always suspicious of traders and knew that they nearly always had a string
of no account animals, yet those folks would fall over themselves to trade, thinking they could outsmart the trader at his
own game.

One spring, in the middle of the nineties, I set out with an
assortment of eight of the trickiest horses I ever seen in one
outfit. Working west I began swapping until I had gotten rid of
most of these plugs, although in the process I acquired two
horses that were worse than the originals. One was a thirteen-
hundred pound dapple-brown mare and the other a fair-look-
ing eleven hundred pound bay horse. As far as I could see they
appeared passingly good, especially the mare. In fact, she
almost looked too good.

But I didn't see far enough. The bay horse turned out to be
a bull windy. His defect showed up the first hour after I hit the
road. A bull windy is a horse that has spells when he becomes

168

so congested he can't breathe out air. When this occurs you have to stop or they're apt to choke. This bay's nostrils had been plugged to quiet him but he blew them out. I was now forced to take it easy, so my pace became unusually slow.

The next morning I hitched up the mare that I had also traded for to see how she would perform in harness. I soon found out. She started to kick hell out of things before I had time to climb on the seat. I then held her head and managed to get her toned down and out of the harness, although it's a wonder she didn't kick the daylights out of me during the process. I knew then that I had to get rid of those two horses in a hurry.

But I didn't hit a trade until I got to Nance County, and between handling the wheezy bull windy and that hell-bent kicking mare it wasn't a sweet job getting there. Upon arriving I pulled up at a crossroads near a creek and made camp for the night. The next morning, about sun-up, I was cooking breakfast when I heard a loud "whoa" over in the cornfield to the left. I looked over to see what was going on at such an early hour and saw a slick-faced farmer turning his team and cultivator into a corn row. From what I could see, he wasn't exactly a true farmer type. He looked too neat and fresh-shaven. You'd call his appearance scholarly.

He evidently had looked my outfit over as he came down the turning row, for he never cast a glance in my direction as he took off on his row of corn. I watched for a minute or so as his rig dwindled toward the far end of the field. Just a hard working farmer, I thought, who was more industrious than the average.

A few minutes later, when I was putting the finishing touches on a stack of flapjacks, I heard a wagon clattering along the bumpy road to the south. They sure are early risers around here, I thought. It was only a little short of six o'clock. After a few minutes a rig hoved into view carrying a big, rawboned individual who was driving a span of maltese-colored mules hitched to a weather-beaten lumber wagon. As he drew abreast of me I noticed he had his mules rigged out with scissors bits and lines that were double-hitched from harness to bridles. That, to a horseman, meant that these mules were hard to manage.

The fellow eyed me in the narrow, suspicious way many farmers were wont to do with strangers. Then his attention shifted to the dapple-brown mare and I thought I could detect a gleam of interest in his deep-set eyes.

As he pulled up with his mules he hailed me in a rumbling, deep-throated voice, "Howdy, stranger. Come far?"

"Quite a piece," I answered.

This was a formal greeting of the times for opening a conflab that usually led up to a trade dickering.

"Swapping a little, I take it," he continued, which of course was an easy conjecture on his part, since my layout had "horse trader" sticking out all over it. His piercing eyes traveled over that dapple-brown mare.

"Little ganted up, ain't she?" he persisted. "You had ought to have a good team like these here mules of mine."

"Well, friend," I told him, "I don't cotton much to mules. They're too tricky."

"This here span ain't," he replied. "Gentle as kittens, they is." He must have thought I was a simpleton, or else he forgot about those scissors bits and double-hitched lines.

Well, we sparred around for quite a spell, but I noticed he kept a tight line on his mules. I had the bull windy hobbled out and of course he didn't look bad when taking it easy. Anyway, I had plugs in his nostrils to silence his breathing. Just to sort of upset him a little, I said, "Your mules a little frisky? I see you got 'em curbed pretty well."

"Oh, no," he replied. "Just a fool notion of mine, using these bridles I got for a couple of wild broncos."

The scholarly appearing farmer with a corn plow came into view on the return leg of his round and drew up directly opposite us. He got down to fiddle around with his cultivator. Since our conversation was carried on in loud tones, much after the fashion of farmers talking to one another across an eighty-acre field, he couldn't help but hear what was said. I figured he was curious to listen in on what he surmised must be a horse trade in the making.

170

And that's just what it was too. My raw-boned friend liked the look of the daple-brown mare, although he tried to give me the opposite impression.

I was still tempted to rib him about the mules. They had long tails and long manes, which was unusual, since it's the custom to give mules a close trim. "Don't you think your scissors bits are apt to make these mules touchy, they being so gentle, like you say?" I asked him.

"Nope," he came back with. "They're used to it. Why, my daughter rides one or 'tother of 'em every evening to git the cows."

He didn't ask me anything about my string, but I figured that he was pretty much interested in my dapple-brown mare. We finally got down to business, with the trade centered on his span of mules, my bull windy and the kicking brown mare. I noticed that the cultivating farmer in the adjacent field lingered around, listened to our dickering.

Well, I talked the rigid-faced farmer out of thirty-two dollars cash boot, after which the trade was made. He unharnessed the mules and helped me lead them to a tree on the four corners. They seemed a little skittish, but didn't cut any capers, though a mule usually shows his nervousness when he is least expected to.

Since the farmer hadn't asked much about the bull windy and mare, I didn't see fit to go into details. We swapped harness too, and I helped him hitch the bull windy and dapple-brown mare to his wagon. I was expecting the mare to let go with her heels any minute but she didn't. He shucked out the thirty-two dollars, then mounted his spring wagon.

When this farmer was busy shifting himself around, preparatory to driving away, I said, "Listen, that mare kicks some, so I advise you to sit on the left-hand side of the seat." Most drivers of horses, by force of habit, drive from the right-hand side and he had the mare hitched up on the "gee" side. But instead of following my advice he leered at me and said, "Never mind, you won't get this team back by scaring me about kicking."

171

I warned him again, but he just grabbed up a stubby whip and touched the mare, saying, "Good-bye. You're talking to the wrong man this time."

He had only gone about twenty-five feet when the mare hung back, causing the farmer to bring his whip into action again. The bull windy, now excited, blew his plugs and commenced to wheeze. The mare, at the same time, began kicking. She kicked out the front end-gate of the wagon and before he could quit the seat she caught it with her heels and upset it, toppling the yelling driver into the wagonbed. Then the mare kicked the wagon tongue loose from the neck yoke, after which she kicked herself out of the harness—all but the short tugs, harness, and collar.

The big, raw-boned farmer swiftly untangled himself from the wagon, after which he took off down the road. His tense face was white as a sheet under his dirty beard. I don't think he stopped running until he got to the next town.

I unhitched the bull windy and the mare and turned them out on the grass in one corner of the crossroads. The cultivating spectator, who had seen the entire occurrence, never said a word as he started up another corn row. As soon as his back was turned, I cached the mules up the road a ways in a ravine.

So there I was with the entire outfit of horses, mules and wagons. I decided to stay, thinking my trader friend would return pretty quick, gunning for trouble. As I had suspected, he did, and brought a deputy sheriff with him. The deputy, puffed up with the importance of his job, wanted to know where the mules were.

I said, "I sold 'em."

"Who to?" he asked.

"I don't know. I'm a stranger around here."

Then he wanted to know what I intended to do about it.

"About what?" I asked him.

"Why, about this outlaw horse trade," he answered.

"It's no outlaw horse trade," I reminded him, "and I don't want the team back."

He said if I didn't do something he would have to arrest me.

172

"Well," I told him, "I've got other stuff I will trade him but I don't want that team back."

The farmer now cussed and said he wouldn't trade with me no how. He was getting his courage back with the officer there, and so he demanded my arrest.

The deputy decided to arrest me, but I advised him to get a warrant first. I thought he would have to go back to town for that. But instead of doing that, his next move was entirely unexpected. He went to the farmer in the adjoining field, who had stopped his rig opposite us after completing another round of cultivating. That scholarly-looking farmer stroked his chin, as if in deep meditation, then beckoned the rest of us to come over. Along with his farming he was also a local justice of the peace. He didn't have a blank warrant, but the deputy had one that the judge, still seated on his plow, signed.

But instead of serving the warrant the whole outfit started for town, leaving me in charge of the stock. I learned afterward that the deputy would have had to hire someone to do this and keep me at his house besides, there being no local jail. The cornfield judge had ordered them to appear the following morning at ten o'clock in the field by the four corners. He evidently didn't want to let a mere court trial interfere with his corn cultivating.

That next morning the deputy and complaining witness showed up and the deputy formally arrested me. A sizeable group of curious people, the sort that are always around trials, trailed the county sheriff and the alleged victim of my criminal exploits in horse trading.

As the hour of the trial was almost at hand, we merely had to wait until the judge hove into sight. After finishing cultivating a corn row, he halted at the end of the field just a few feet from the gnarled trunk of a fallen cottonwood tree. We filed into the "court room" and seated ourselves on the fallen tree—that is, all who found room to squeeze in.

The judge called the court to order by tapping the metal frame of his cultivator with an alligator wrench. He remained sitting on the cultivator while his horses, not much interested in court procedure, made futile efforts to lower their heads enough, despite the check reins, to nip off the young tender corn shoots.

The black-visaged farmer rose to his feet and voiced his complaint, laying it on pretty thick and making me out seven kinds of liar, horse thief, and all-round dangerous character. His name was Barten Feazzle, and somehow or other it fitted his person.

There was no prosecuting attorney there, but none apparently was needed, since the deputy and his witness seemed to be handling the prosecution in a very able manner. The court had no official docket, although I wondered idly why he didn't rig up his traveling cultivator court room with regulation court room equipment. The deputy however produced two used envelopes which were blank on the back side, even if a trifle smeared with thumb prints, and these served as the official record of the trial.

The farmer must have known that the judge himself had seen and heard the trade, but in the present excitement he had probably forgotten it. Anyway, he, like most people on their own dunghill, thought that I, being a stranger, would get the worst end of the deal.

The judge, as he listened to the scourching indictment, kicked at a tangle of roots on one of the cultivator shovels. Then he spoke in a crisp, curt voice, injecting a surprising amount of dignity and sterness into his demeanor. Seeing as how the whole affair was a sort of a farce and entirely lacking in courtroom setting or formality, I was somewhat amused and a little disgusted. This country squire, I figured, would give me the short end of the stick.

"Your name is Croughan, is it not?"

"Yes, your honor," I answered with just a shade of humbleness and awe, knowing from experience that a judge is always impressed by a respectful salutation.

His slick, pallid face reminded me of a confirmed poker player. His countenance was inscrutable. "What is your occupation, Mr. Croughan?" he continued.

"Horse trader," I told him. "A traveling trader."

He looked a trifle blank, then said, "Well, that's putting it rather neatly. But after all, I suppose it's a profession in a way."

No legal formalities were being abided by, and the judge seated on his cultivator seat did all the questioning. His team stood remarkably quiet and disinterested. It looked like they had experienced other such sessions in their work-day routine.

The judge made one remark that was amusing when he said, "This case is being tried on its own merits and without benefit of counsel." I thought he had taken that out of a book somewhere. "Witness for the prosecution, please take the stand," he ordered. The stand was literal enough, for Feazzle just rose up from the log and rested his bony length on his enormous feet, which were planted in a corn row.

The judge fixed a cold eye on him as he said, "Mr. Feazzle, this might be a little out of order, but if you can recollect, you will recall I was around when you and this horse trader, or whatever he calls himself, dickered to make the trade of your mules for his horses. Just what is your complaint, anyway? Did he misrepresent?"

Feazzle hemmed and hawed, and then blurted out, "This here tramp hoss trader well nigh got me killed with his kicking hellion of a mare."

"But, Mr. Feazzle, didn't he warn you not to sit on the right-hand side of the seat? Isn't that a fact?" The judge here muttered in an undertone about being sure he had heard me say that.

"I dunno' about that," Feazzle stammered. "I can't remember."

"Well, didn't you then tell him he was barking up the wrong tree, and that he needn't worry about you?" the judge persisted.

Feazzle looked blank and mumbled something about the danged trader being too nosey.

The judge, now thoroughly warmed up, continued to grill the squirming Feazzle, "Didn't you tell the defendant that your little girl rode one of these mules after the cows every night?"

175

His honor didn't even bother to wait for an answer to that one. He went on, "I'll bet you fifty dollars there isn't a grown man in this county that can ride one of those mules bareback."

"The other horse was a wind choker too," Feazzle retorted. He evidently had some knowledge of a bull windy.

The judge then looked in my direction and announced his decision. "Mr. Croughan, you're acquitted. And you, Mr. Feazzle, are assessed with the costs of this case. That will be a dollar and fifty cents, and kindly remove your team and wagon from the people's highway. Court is adjourned."

Feazzle now looked like a dog that had been caught sucking eggs. He was afraid to go near the mare he had bargained for, so asked me if I would take both the mare and bull windy off his hands. Meantime, he paid the judge the costs, who, upon pocketing it, chirped to his horses and took off down the field.

The crowd of spectators scattered, and the deputy strode disgustedly to his rig and drove away.

Well, I felt a little sorry for Feazzle, so gave him two bulldog revolvers, a Waterbury watch, and two dollars and a half for the bull windy and the kicking mare. He gave me a bill of sale, then set off toward town to get another team to hitch up to his wagon. I picked up the mules that had been cached in the ravine and went on my way.

A few days on the road toned them down a bit and I dealt them later for a light team of six-year-olds and fifty dollars in cash boot. I traded off the bull windy and dapple-brown mare on a farmer who had recently been appointed road overseer and wanted a couple extra horses to work on a road drag.

I told him the mare was a little touchy in the heels, but he just laughed and said most of them were. I sold them to him outright for one hundred and fifteen dollars and was mighty glad to be rid of the two. He grinned as he handed me the money, remarking exuberantly, "That brown mare is worth the money alone, if I don't miss my guess."

I wondered if he'd changed his mind later, but I didn't linger around to find out.

176

Coming into Glanders in a Bad Way

There can be little doubt that a lot of horse-trading tricks backfired. Sometimes a man could trick his way into a trade that left him holding the reins of a useless snide. But only the winner of such a trade would be willing to pass such a story along, and even he might be reluctant to spread the story if he wanted to keep his trick secret.

It is unusual, then, to get a story like this one, where a trading trick did indeed backfire. The Federal Writers Project files contain information about neither the narrator nor collector of the tale.

There was a horse trading farmer in our territory by the name of Hank Bevins who was tricky as all get out. I had no particular reason in wanting to bugher him up on a trade except that he was pretty well up on all the horse trading tricks, although he was no crawfisher if a deal went wrong.

The horse trading trick I shall now relate is most effective in a locality where there has been a glanders scare. There had been one or two cases of glanders reported in the neighborhood, so the setting for this particular stunt was ideal. You see, if at the time of a trade you put a drop or two of carbolic acid on the little white spot that shows in a horse's nostrils, he will look like he had glanders, distemper, and everything else the next morning. His nose will run mucus all over the place and usually he'll stand and rub his nose on the feed box or manger all night.

Well, for the fun of it, I wished to try out this trick on Hank. So I went over to Hank's place with a mare I didn't care much about and we got to talking trade. As trades go, it wasn't much except that two horses were involved in the deal—if you would call them that.

Anyway, we traded, and while Hank was busy picking out the poorest halter on the place to throw in with his horse I gave my mare a little touch of carbolic acid in her nostrils. Then, leading Hank's horse I made tracks in a hurry.

177

I didn't expect to see him after that, for he usually stuck by a trade, good, bad, or indifferent. But the next day, about noon, he showed up leading my mare. I happened to be around and was a little surprised, for Hank didn't have the reputation of kicking back on a deal.

He wasn't mad, just excited. I knew what was up, all right, but he hurried to tell me about it. That mare, he said, was sure comin' into the glanders in a bad way. Her nose was still running a stream.

"Well, what do you want me to do about it?" I asked him. "We traded, didn't we?"

"W-w-w-why," he stuttered, "I ain't figurin' to have you do anything."

I was so surprised at this turn of affairs things had taken that for once I was at a loss. I was between the devil and the deep blue sea. If I told him about the trick, since it was one he didn't know about, he would probably fly off the handle, and yet if I didn't, he was sure to spread the news that my string of horses had the glanders.

He wouldn't take his horse back neither, when I offered it to him, so I just had to let him leave the mare and tell him I'd watch her a while and let him know.

Of course she was all right in no time. I let him know about my trick later and offered to let him have her back. But he wouldn't have it that way, declaring that it was his own blunder in getting all fired up about nothing.

The Heaves Story

But, on the other hand, there is no shortage of tales of slick traders being tricked and deceived with their own medicine, as is the case in this next example. There is no information available regarding the teller or collector of the story.

178

Horses afflicted with heaves are common and many of them fall into the hands of traders. Ordinarily the traders know it, but they could drive such hard deals that it was often advantageous to trade in them. A heavey horse generally shows the defect by the quivering and pulsing at the region just ahead of the flanks. Another sign is found in the nostrils, which almost become square.

Heaves is caused by infected or irritated lungs. Tincture of lobelia and oil-of-tar will temporarily keep the heaves in check, although I doubt that this remedy would fool an expert.

One time I made a trade with an Irish neighbor named Denny. When we got together he tried to work off a bay horse that didn't look just right. I felt sure his animal was heavey. I didn't want to trade because I brought along some of my better stock, which was fairly sound and smooth. You see, I had come with the expectation of giving the Irishman a middling-good trade because he was a neighbor of mine. So I left my poorer trading stock at home.

Denny naturally tried to stampede me into a quick trade, but I held him off by protesting that neither of my horses was up to his and I didn't want to put out any boot. In a few days I went back to Denny's place. This time I took along my heavey animal, now temporarily fixed up with the oil-of-tar treatment.

Old Denny, after eyeing the heavey horse from every angle, seemed satisfied, although I didn't think he knew much about horses. My horse was the better looker, but wasn't worth a continental for anything but trading. The Irishman's horse, for that matter, wasn't much either. Well, we traded, but I did it more for the fun of the thing, thinking Denny might raise a little hell when he caught on to the fact that I had done to him what he was out to do to me.

And sure enough, he came over in a few days with blood in his eyes. "Ye dommed thievin' hound," he sputtered, "the likes of you ought to be locked in the calaboose!"

"Now, now, Denny, don't be so hard on me. The horse you traded me was just as bad, if not worse, than the one you got from me."

179

"Oi don't give a damn if he was. The loikes of you turned me a devil's plague when you give me a pack of lies about yer plugs, just so's you could work off that no good scout of a broke-down pelter."

Denny was mad, mostly because of the way I had put him off and then switched my heavey animal on him. I told him we'd trade back, but the old rascal demanded his horse back and ten dollars cash. Eventually we did exchange horses, but he didn't get the ten dollars.

He Isn't a Kicker, Is He?

"Doctoring one's own horse to facilitate a profitable exchange was obviously standard horse-trading procedure; on some rare occasions, however, a trader would have an opportunity to doctor his opponent's horse so that it would appear to be a poor risk at best—to the owner's bewilderment. Strictly speaking, such behavior was considered dishonest, even in terms of the very liberal morality of the traders' code.

The Federal Writers Project files contain no information about the following story, but its style and language suggest that it was one of Lew Croughan's and was therefore probably collected by Harold J. Moss.

There was not much fun in being too serious in a trade if you knew a trick or two that would liven things up.

One day I drove into a farmer's place whose owner was known to be tighter than the bark on a tree. I had a big, black horse with me who was a little stiff from too much road work, but, taken all around, wasn't a bad trade.

The old geezer was out puttering around his barn when I pulled in, but wouldn't hardly look up. I'd heard he wanted a bigger field horse to match one he had on hand and, anyway, I wanted to have a little fun with him.

180

After a while he warmed up and even began showing signs of being interested. Pretty soon he disappeared into the barn, after which he came out leading a fair looking bay that was redder than any horse I'd ever seen. He even offered to show him off and the horse seemed to perform in good shape.

"He isn't a kicker, is he?" I asked, innocent enough, for I was leading up to something. "No sirree, he's nothing of the sort," the old boy shot back at me.

Now there's ways to make a horse cut up and kick. The best of these is to rub carbon-bisulphide on a horse's rump. It makes him so wild that he's apt to kick like the devil. So, after getting the horse harnessed, I led him around and looked him over till I got a chance, without being noticed, to pour a little of that stinking stuff on the horse's rump. It doesn't work where there's no hair, but poured on the hair it burns like hell. If you rub it on a horse's belly, he'll act as if he had the colic.

Well, the stuff soaked in and started to burn and that bay just naturally had a fit. His eyes got wild, he trembled all over and then started to jump and kick. The old farmer just stood and stared with his mouth agape and his scraggly whiskers waving in the wind. He didn't get a whiff of the stinking stuff, so he couldn't know what had happened. I had a time hanging on to that plunging, kicking bay horse, but I managed. The burning and itching soon began to ease off and the horse quieted down, though he was still uneasy.

The bay's flabbergasted owner was speechless. Finally he ventured, "Guess something's sticking him."

"You sure he isn't a kicker?" I asked him, but I wanted to laugh.

The workout showed the bay was really pretty sound at that, so we traded, with the old tightwad handing over fifteen dollars cash boot. I don't think he would have ever done that if it hadn't been for the kicking trick.

In Her Cups

And certainly the sweetest trade was the one in which the deception was discovered before the closing of the deal. Then the loser was so embarrassed that he would make almost any deal, and the winner usually enjoyed a monetary gain as well as an ample bonus of self-satisfaction and righteousness, enough certainly to cover up any guilt about his own deception.

The story was collected from Lew Croughan by Harold J. Moss on 13 February 1941.

It was a tacky looking outfit that approached my road side camp just out of Germantown [now Garland, Nebraska] some thirty years ago. A dull, pulpy faced man was framed in the open front of a dirty canvas covered wagon which was drawn by two "ganted-up" plugs of horses. Several other discouraged looking nags trailed the wagon. Among them was a brown mare, which seemed to have some difficulty in keeping up, even at the slow pace the outfit was moving.

He pulled up, of course, and stared at me. I knew him, all right—it was a tin horn trader from down around Fairbury, a fellow by the name of Stokes. He knew me too, but he seemed to have difficulty in placing me. When I hailed him by name, however, he brightened up and returned the greeting, though without much enthusiasm. I expected that he had in mind making a trade too. Horse traders, you know, could hardly pass one another up without some kind of a trade. They were always ambitious to out-do one another, although personally, I never had too much luck that way.

Well, after he got his outfit spotted and taken care of, we talked about this and that and looked over each other's horses, but nothing was mentioned about trading particularly. Finally I asked him about that brown mare; he had just put her out on grass. I had a reason in doing so, but we'll come to that later.

He looked at me funny like. "Croughan,"—he tried to make his voice sound doubly sincere—"I've never traded with

182

you and so I'm a goin' to give you the deal of your life. In fact, I'm goin' to give you the best of it. That brown mare there, I traded a black for, that sold later for a hundred twenty-five dollars, and the man turned right around and offered me twenty-five dollars for my bargain back. I wouldn't take it either, so you know how good that mare is. I can even show you a man who offered me a hundred and fifty dollars for her just two days ago."

Stokes was lying like hell and what got me was that he was thick-headed enough to think that I would swallow any such guff. The mare wasn't a bad looker but I heard her wheezing like a wind-broke horse when he pulled up by my outfit. He kept right on telling me how good she was. In fact, he gave a pretty fair sales talk without any regard for the truth whatsoever.

He had his eye on a four-year-old bay in my string, a pretty little horse about twelve hundred pounds and without a blemish, but I'd hardly have valued it at one hundred and fifty dollars, or even one hundred and twenty-five. He proposed an even trade, and when I asked him how old his brown was, he said, "Well, she still has her cups," meaning she wasn't over nine years old.

It was a good opening to have a little fun with him, so I said, "Yeah, I ought to know; I burned cups in her teeth not so long ago."

We do that, you know, once in a while with a little acid or something, the cups being the black rings in the center of the grinding surface of the teeth. They disappear about the ninth year and then the horse is known as smooth-mouthed.

Well, you could of knocked him over with a feather as he gaped at me. His pulpy face sort of froze like. "Y-y-you must be mistaken, Mr. Croughan," he stuttered. "The man I got this mare from said he'd owned her all his life. She was out of his best mare and so he knew her age and she wasn't smooth-mouthed."

I had to laugh and his face which was naturally the color of putty turned beet red. "Now, Stokes,"—I decided to tell him the story of that bay mare—"Five days ago I traded this bay

183

mare you have there to a farmer down by Pleasant Dale for a little burro and a little Jennie, a seven-dollar Elgin watch, and a dollar cash, which was pretty good considering that she's got the heaves and is going on seventeen. Of course she's not worth all that, but since, as you say, we've never traded before, I'm going to give you the best of it. I'll give you the Elgin watch and the dollar for that bay mare. I think I ought to have the little burro and Jennie for my trouble."

He was pretty red faced, but it was a sort of angry red by now. "You're trying to roup me, Croughan. You must have your horses mixed up."

"All right," I told him. "Of course I'm not trying anything of the sort. You can take the deal or leave it, whichever way you want to jump. But that mare is so heavey I know she'll wheeze herself apart if she moves fast for ten rods."

I'd found that out already and yet I admired the man's colossal gall in trying to get away with such an impossible bluff. He'd found out the mare was no good and would hardly keep to the road long, so I guess he had the foolish idea that he could unload her at some fantastic price.

Well, he just stood there and looked at me some more, a little glary at first but gradually turning sheepish. He wanted to know then where the burro and Jennie were and I told him I sold them for a dollar a piece. That wasn't quite right, as I actually traded them for a pretty fair little black mare, which I had just sold for twenty dollars a day or so before.

He was over his confusion and mad by now and with a sickly grin he admitted that he did get the bay mare from that same farmer but he said, "I give him fifty dollars for her." That might possibly have been true, for he was a sort of a chump.

He finally took the watch and the dollar. I traded that bay for a big black, smooth-mouthed mule with sore shoulders and after the whole transaction I was ahead a good leather collar and seven dollars and fifty cents in cash.

That's the trader's life for you—lots of fun as well as grief, especially when you run into a fellow like Stokes, who tries to put through such a cock-eyed deal.

Part IV: *RACERS*

Old Parity

Horses were vehicles of personal or family pride, and of course they had the additional practical applications as work animals and the power for transportation. Horses were bought and traded on their beauty or their suitability to the work of the plow or reliability of the carriage.

But there was another consideration, too—speed. Not speed at work or transport, but pure and simple speed. Then as now, speed was a mania for some, and no community social occasion could be considered complete without horse races. Even today in some Plains villages celebrations must include horse races. One small town I am familiar with consistently refuses to pave its main street because it would hamper the annual races on the Fourth of July.

Most traders had at least a passing interest in racing stock; some, like Ike Ault, spent their whole lives and energies looking for the fast ones. The Federal Writers Project files contained no information for this tale other than Ault's name.

If they hadn't invented those high-power motors, nor discovered gasoline, we all wouldn't be living in a world at war today. They got to have trouble in order to test the strength of those new inventions, take it out on the population of countries. The world is traveling too fast for me anymore. I wonder what it will be like a couple of hundred years from now. The horse and buggy days were good enough for me, lived peaceful, simple, never had much but was satisfied.

I was born in Illinois, sixty seven years ago, came out here when I was four years old with my parents, who bought an eighty-acre tract of land two and a half miles west of Beatrice, Nebraska. Later, in about five years, father bought the other eighty adjoining acres and together we had a quarter section.

187

We had a pretty tough struggle for a few years, but that all goes with it. I always was fond of horses, and when I reached the age of twenty I kinda took it in my head to get me some race horses.

It started with my Indian pony, which I thought was pretty fast for a short distance. There was a neighbor boy who had a sorrel filly and we had a matched race for a prize of my saddle against his twelve dollars and a half, for a quarter of a mile, down the road from a standing start.

I guess everyone in the neighborhood heard about it and were on hand the day of the race. We selected a couple of judges, a starting judge, and a finishing judge. I guess I won by half a length.

Father got wind of it, and he was deadly against betting, being very religious. Told me if I was going to race horses I would have to go on my own, as he wanted no part of it. I decided to quit for the present, but always had it on my mind. Racing horses was my one and almost only thought.

I managed to acquire a broken down race mare from someone of whom I don't remember the name now, but anyway, there was a stud imported from France that was retired for stud duty over at Fairbury. I pleaded with the man to breed my mare and after a few attempts and negative answers, he finally gave in and out of that mating I got a fine little colt, named her Nettie.

I was awfully proud of that colt, practically lived with it. When she was a two-year-old I broke her to ride. She was the gentlest thing if there ever was one, had no trouble at all breaking her. I could see at the very start that she loved to run.

In the meantime I had acquired another race mare and a gelding, not so good, just a little below the average. Got acquainted with the Wallace family at Fairbury, who raised horses—three boys, Al, Bill, and Red. Al is night clerk at the Sam Lawrence hotel and he was some jockey in his day, which I will tell you about later. Red has spent his life around race tracks. I haven't seen him for two years, but the last I heard, he was at Sportsman Park in Chicago. I want to tell you a

188

little story about Red that happened only three years ago out here at the Fairgrounds in 1938 at the fall race meeting.

I hadn't seen Red for a few years and the first of August that year I was sitting in a tavern trying to separate my tongue from the top of my mouth with a cool glass of suds when someone slapped me on the back and says, "If it ain't my old partner Ike. How's the old boy anyway? Watcha doin' now?" And kept firing questions so fast I didn't have time to answer any of them.

He ordered two more of the amber fluid and Red started in to let me in on a secret. "Ike," he says, "we're going to clean up at this race meet this year and I know you have always been good at keeping things to yourself, and I'm going to tell you somethin'. You see, I just blew in from Chicago last night with a horse. Cost me seventy-five dollars to have a man haul him here in a van. You remember old Parity? The Whitneys used to own him and won a lot of big races in the east with him. Well, he broke down and I had a man in Chicago buy him and turn him over to me to ride. Had him fired last winter." ["Fired" means a veterinary pokes the flesh to the bone with an electric needle to relieve the inflammation in the ankle up to the knee, gives it a chance to mend.]

"Worked him out at Sportsman Park and he is as sound as a dollar again. He's out to the gounds now, and I'm prepping him for the Nebraska Derby. Probably start him once before the Derby to win a purse to reimburse me so I can get some folding money to lay on him in the Derby. Come on out in a few days, old partner, and watch him work out in the morning."

Always did work and train their horses at the crack of dawn.

I went out in about a week and Red got a boy to gallop him twice around the track, then we put the stop watch on him and clocked his time. The last half mile—believe it or not—he worked in forty seconds, and that is plenty fast for a half mile track. That convinced me that Red really had something. I started saving my money to clean up the first time he started in a race.

189

Time went on and he seemed to get better with every workout. Come August 28 and the races started. After the first week Red entered Parity in a race, one mile flat for horses of all ages. He got a jockey to ride, carrying only one hundred and ten pounds, which looked like a cinch to get down to that finish line on top. I believe it was the sixth race our cinch was entered in.

Come time for "Old Parity's" colors to fly down in front, I could see Red bringing our steed out of the barn, from the other side of the track, walked him to the Paddock, where he was saddled, and Red gave his instructions to the jockey on how to ride him.

The bugle sounded, and that means the horses are coming out on the track to parade for a while, while the suckers shove their two dollar bets through the mutuel windows. Parity opened on the probable odds board at ten to one, which was a fair price for a cinch.

As the horses were headed for the starting gate, here comes Red stumbling up towards the judges' stand on the inside of the track to watch his great wizard of speed leave the others in amazement.

I says, "Red, what do you think?"

He says, "Go in there and buy all the tickets you got money for and don't even look back, as it's in the bag."

I says, "Red, do you really think he'll win?"

"Win hell? How far can you throw a claw hammer from a sitting position?"

"Well," says I, "quite a ways."

"Well, that's how far he'll win by."

I'm convinced, and so is Red, as he hands me his last sawbuck to bet right on his nose. I had eighteen dollars, every cent I had in the world. I bet ten dollars to win and eight dollars to show. A little protection, I thought, as there is a thousand ways to lose a horse race and only one way to win one, and that is to get under that wire first.

As I fought my way out of the crowd down to the fence to get a first-class view of the race, the announcer says over the

190

PA system, then, "All in line," drops his red flag, and the starter releases the electric gate and they are off.

"At the quarter it's Parity by a half. June Bird second a length, Silver Bell third, Jinx is laying fourth." I thought, "Okay, it's a cinch."

They go around the track twice for a mile race, and at the half mile three horses passed him. I thought he was taking him back to save his wind for the final drive for home, and still wasn't uneasy. But as they rounded the far turn for home, our Parity was far back and at the finish Parity was just coming around the upper far turn. Finished a dead last by two blocks.

There was I, busted on a cinch. I says to Red, "What happened?"

Red says, "I guess he turned out to be a morning glory"— that is a horse that works like lightning in the morning but won't run a lick in a race.

I guess them Whitneys knew what they were doing when they got rid of him. I think Red sold him for a saddle pony for twenty-five dollars. He was sure mad. I haven't seen him since.

Well, getting back to my racing experience, I took Nettie and the other three horses that spring to the races. They had a Nebraska circuit at that time. Had about fifteen race meets in Nebraska at different towns at Old Settlers meetings, fairs, and so forth.

I got my "tack" in shape and Al Wallace, the jockey from Fairbury, came along to ride my horses. Our first meet was at Falls City.

On the way down we passed by a farmer friend of mine's farm house, so we put up for the night there. He had a horse that he said could run a little and told me I could take him along and make what I could out of him if he did any good. So I thought I might as well as my farmer friend was a horse trader on the side and knew his horses pretty well. He didn't look like he could run but I hitched him behind the wagon and we started out for Falls City.

I'll swear we hadn't gone but about ten miles and that horse started to limp bad. I sure thought I had a lemon but we continued on and when we arrived at Falls City we got stalls

191

for our horses, bedded them down for the night, and went to bed. We had a stall next to the horses which we slept in. Always slept in the barn in the summer. It wasn't so bad, only had to fight the flies, which were always hungry.

There was a Gypsy with a covered wagon load of kids and the old lady parked over in the center field. He had a few horses. You know at that time there were always Gypsies in the country who would choose the local boys for a horse race.

One morning I was going through the center field and got talking with the Gyp. He says, "I sure would like to find someone who thinks he's got a horse that he thinks can run for a quarter mile."

I says, "Well, Gyp, I picked up a cripple along the way that I think can beat anything you got."

He says, "Where is he?"

So I goes over to the barn and leads him over, and he was limping all the way.

The Gyp says, "I can beat him with the poorest of my lot easy." He cracks, "How much you want to bet?"

I says, "Make it easy on yourself."

The Gyp took invoice and says. "I'll bet you twenty-five dollars."

That's okay with me, so the Gyp says, "If I can't beat that broken-down bone pile I'll leave town before night."

You know that old horse was funny. When you put a saddle on him he would perk right up and look like a neat race animal. He limped by nature.

The Gyp says for me to pick out any one of my horses I cared to, but I refused because I told him to run the best one he had, as I didn't want him to have any alibis. He had two horses that were identical. Looked like twins. He selected one of them.

He had one of his kids ride his horse and Al was up on mine. The agreement was from a walk up start to the wire, then let go. Al got the old horse in a good position and was the far superior rider than his boy and got about a length the best of it at the start and finished about a good half length in front at the finish.

192

The Gyp paid off the twenty-five dollars. I took the old horse over to the barn, walked him around for half an hour to cool him out, put him back in his stall, and started out of the barn to go to town, when I see a wagon approach me, and sure enough it was the Gyp who pulled stakes, says, "Ike, I'm keeping my word. I told you if I couldn't beat an old broken-down horse like that I'd leave town before night and so here I go."

I hollered back, "You just as well, as there is lots better horses than that one around here."

He asked me if I wanted to sell the good race runner. I told him that he didn't belong to me, but I thought he could buy him from John Hodges over at Homesville, the owner. The Gyp happened to know him and said he would stop and see, but I don't know whether he ever did, cause I asked John when I took him back if he did and he never saw him, so I don't know whether he ever did later or not. He just as well traded all the stock for one fair runner as the ones he had were not much good.

Al and I stayed there for the duration of the meet but only got to start one of our horses once and he finished second, so we didn't do so good there. We would work them out and got Nettie in swell shape, and I knew she was going to develop into a good race mare.

We pulled stakes then and took our stock to Auburn. I believe it was for the county fair. There was some trotting and pacing races scheduled and also about ten running mares. There was a race made for non-winners and first starters in the three year class in which I entered Nettie.

They started them at that time from a wire stretched across the track with a release spring that the starter would release when they started them. Al, of course, was up on Nettie and she acted like an old campaigner at the post, just stood there, kinda pawing the ground, itching to run, and I want to tell you, when that starter let them go, Nettie shot out of there and was three lengths in front coming by the stands and not another horse gained on her. She just widened on them at every eighth mile and finally won by five lengths. Al said after the race it was all he could do to hold her. I believe that purse paid one hundred and fifty dollars. My first race winnings at the track, and was I proud. Boy, it sure gave me a thrill to see a horse that I had owned and trained and raised from a colt to do like she did. We made about seven meets that summer and when I pulled back home I had about six hundred dollars saved. I ran Nettie for three seasons and she only finished twice other than first. Once second and once out of the money—fifth, I believe.

My father kept wanting me to quit racing and my wife was pregnant and insisted I quit, so I decided to sell the racing stock and equipment in order to get along with everyone. I sure hated to sell Nettie, as she had certainly been an ace in the hole for me. I had learned to almost love that animal, as she was certainly a thoroughbred.

It seems like I was nervous and not satisfied after I quit racing, and went back to farming. Wasn't much excitement, too slow, just work from morning till night. See crop failures once in a while but not as frequent as now, but anyway, when a fellow labors hard and works his head off for a whole year planting, cultivating, and getting crops to growing good, then along comes some hot winds, grasshoppers or something to destroy all you have done in a few days, I tell you, it takes a lot of courage to face these reverses from time to time.

The Famous Shooting Star

But the business of trading racers was even more risky than the course of the usual trader's activities because a nag that could not run usually wasn't much good for anything else either. Therefore, the wife of the race-horse trader was usually even testier than that of the regular trader. His life rarely lacked for

194

interest. This tale was collected from Lew Croughan on 22 January 1941, by Harold J. Moss.

Bill Coats was most certainly not a race track type. He was too drab and colorless, one of those dull-looking individuals who would pass almost unnoticed anywhere, his one hundred and sixty pound, slouching figure and slack features presenting none of those abstract qualities which might fire the imagination or create a flicker of interest. He lived at Beatrice, along in the early 1900's, where he had managed to acquire a Bohemian wife, who had several thousand dollars in her own right.

It was during a visit to the state fair at Lincoln that Bill got the race horse bug, mostly because he surreptitiously listened in on the supposedly private conversation of a couple of fairly smooth looking strangers. These two were ranged alongside of Bill watching the workout of several harness horses over the fence at the quarter mile stretch. They talked in low tones, their voices hushed as if they were guarding some very valuable secret. However, it was no trouble for Bill to hear every word and get the hang of their semi-whispered talk. They looked like authentic race horse men all right—all decked out in race track checked suits, while one carried a horse blanket folded over his arm.

Bill's interest in the track work-out shifted to the two strangers' discussion. If they had any idea that he was listening in, they most surely did not indicate it. In fact, he could just as well have been a thousand miles away for all the notice they accorded him.

"This horse I'm telling you about is over in number three barn and he's a natural and in the money," the taller of the two almost hissed as he lowered his voice a couple of notches further down the scale. "He can be bought for three hundred and fifty dollars, not a cent less, and the man that gets him can clean up. A fellow by the name of Woodsley owns him, but he's too dumb to know what he's got."

Now Bill, ordinarily none too enterprising nor endowed with even commonplace visionary powers, found himself enthusiastically considering the possibilities of race horse own-

195

ership and the easy money it seemed to involve. Besides, it promised a more or less facinating round of interesting experiences and what was even more intriguing, such a business seemed to point to a life of comparative ease, a thing that would be delightfully acceptable to the none too energetic Bill.

He sidled away from the two strangers and hot footed it for the barn numbered three. Had he bothered to look around, he might have noticed something more or less significant in the behavior of the two. As he eased away, they both ceased talking rather abruptly and the taller of the two closed one eye and grinned slyly at his partner. Then they strolled off but in another direction from Bill.

Upon reaching the barn, Bill strolled in, pretending a casualness he did not in the least feel. A suspicious attendant promptly inquired what he had on his mind, but the subtle Bill only mumbled something about "lookin' over the horses." There weren't too many animals stabled in this particular barn and he was a little disappointed; furthermore, none of these looked even to his impracticed eye as any too promising. After poking around for some time, he became somewhat impatient and decided to make a discreet inquiry of the surly attendant, whose eyes were set a trifle too close together, while his ears lay almost flat against his skull.

Still affecting an attitude of indifference, Bill casually asked him if he ever run across any good harness horses which might be for sale. The attendant, after studying Bill for a half a minute, rubbed his stubby forefinger along his narrow nose and cautiously answered by asking a question: "What makes you think I'd know of any such race track stock?"

Bill, now entering into the spirit of answering a question by asking one, put one to him: "Do you happen to know a man by the name of Woodsley?"

The stableman gave a slight start and peered closer at his questioner: "Well, I might and I might not. That depends."

Bill sensed that this dodging of the issue might continue indefinitely, but it served to add an air of mystery to the thing and whetted his interest still further. "Well, I just thought I'd ask. No harm in that, I guess."

196

The stablehand appeared to reconsider and finally grudgingly admitted that a Mr. Woodsley did have a small string of race horses, several of which he had around for the fair races. "He ought to be along in a little while. He has one of his horses here now, but I can't let you go near the horse until Woodsley shows up. You know a lot of tricks are pulled in this business."

Well, Woodsley—if that was his name—showed up and his puny figure suggested that he might have been a professional jockey himself at some time, or even right at the time. He listened to the clumsy feeler Bill put out about maybe picking up a track horse or two, and his face seemed to assume a wooden expression so common to veterans of the gambling profession.

"Where," he asked, "did you hear about me?"

There it was again, answering a question by asking another. Bill must have thought that the race track crowd was a canny outfit indeed.

He was a little reluctant to say just how he had heard Woodsley's name mentioned, so he just said, a little vaguely, that he'd heard of him around the track and of course that was the truth, but not in detail.

The two strangers certainly were not in evidence and by this time Bill was thoroughly convinced that they had been sincere in their confidential discussion of what looked like a good thing. Woodsley, it's true, acted a little queer, but that only acted as a build-up of the proposition as far as Bill was concerned. Finally the cautious Woodsley agreed to show Bill around and leading him to the rear of the stable he opened the door of a "box" and motioned inside.

There stood a blazed-faced bay and, although it was a little dark, the animal looked to be of good lines and build, though a trifle rangy. For some reason or other the horse was blanketed although the day was warm and, as far as appearances went, he hadn't had a work-out for some time. The horse, Woodsley said, was the famous Shooting Star, who had made a name for himself back in Illinois.

Bill's racing fever was mounting rapidly and he chose to believe that here was a golden opportunity to get hold of a real

197

money maker. Since he knew very little about horses in general and race horses in particular, it was likely that he was impressed mostly by the two strangers' conversation that he felt sure was not intended for other ears.

Woodsley, once he was warmed up, proved to be a supersalesman, and he soon had Bill thinking that whoever was smart enough to own that horse had a rosy future ahead of him.

Had Bill taken the trouble to examine that animal the way any horseman would have done he might have avoided what happened to him. For one thing, both shanker joints were fired over the hoof and, though the foxy Mr. Woodsley talked in glowing terms about the horse being five-gaited—that's a horse that can change his gait five times in a mile—it turned out that each change was a turn for the worst. As a harness horse chances were that he wasn't even a very good buggy plug. Woodsley probably gave him a hypodermic before the sketchy check-out, which actually did not prove anything at that.

He asked three hundred and fifty dollars all told and intimated that time was passing and he had to know. Now Bill did not have three hundred and fifty dollars and probably never had had such an amount at one time in his whole life, but he knew that his wife had it and he assured Woodsley that he would return the following morning with the money. Returning to Beatrice he lost no time in approaching his wife on the matter, telling her that they would soon be making thousands of dollars on the horse in question.

The wife, who knew nothing about the racing business, had had some experience in money matters and particularly in the way of some of Bill's previous deals, which were not to her way of thinking "howling successes." Then again, her husband had mentioned five hundred dollars for the horse instead of three hundred and fifty, evidently having in mind a little extra capital, without being too explicit about it. Five hundred dollars was a lot of money, but Bill made such an impassioned plea that in the end she agreed to try him and his schemes once more.

Bill hastened back to Lincoln with the money and the race horse passed into his possession without a hitch, although by this time his enthusiasm and eagerness had soared to such a height that he was fearful that Mr. Woodsley would back out on the deal. However, that gentleman proved to be a man of his word—at least in this case, when it served him well to play that part.

Bill took his "prize" to another stable for the day, after paying over his three hundred and fifty dollars to the now quite sociable Woodsley. That afternoon the two strangers, who had unwittingly—or so Bill thought—inspired him to enter the field of racing in the role of an out-and-out owner in fee simple, strolled into the stable and looked around idly. It was, apparently, just a purposeless visit and they didn't give Bill a second look until he approached them, eager to somehow hear more good news about Shooting Star.

The men exchanged meaning glances as Bill led them back and pointed with pride to his newly acquired horse. For a minute or two they just seemed to doubt their eyes and stared unbelievingly at something unreal. "W-w-w-why," stammered the taller of the two, "that's Woodsley's Shooting Star. You don't mean to tell us you own him?!"

"That's right, partners," said the exuberant Bill. "He belongs to me now."

The two seemed lost in thought, which Bill interpreted as bitter disappointment in losing out on such a splendid deal. When the two "authorities" on race horses had recovered from their shock, they lost no time in proposing that they "team up" with Bill and make some of the late county fairs and—so they said—"clean up on the rube suckers."

Bill, still having around one hundred and fifty dollars out of his five hundred—the item he had forgotten to mention to his wife—fell right in with the scheme and after a few preliminary arrangements, the trio and Shooting Star landed out in Thayer County at the annual "punkin show."

Incredibly enough, Bill had not even bothered himself to try out the "five-gaited" Shooting Star and his new partners apparently thought it was unnecessary also. The first day they just occupied themselves getting the lay of the land and watching what races were scheduled. There weren't very many, nor were they anything more than ordinary back-roads affairs.

They managed to enter "Shooting Star" in a mile heat the next day, which was supposed to be a trotting race but turned out to be most anything, with Shooting Star's tendency to follow his multi-gaited performance and break every so often.

Since there was only one other entry and this a sleepy-looking nag, entirely unpromising and which had a gait all his own, the race finished with Bill's horse slightly in the lead. The smaller one of Bill's partners drove the race. Shooting Star failed to demonstrate in that race that he had come from a family of very fast moving "stars" but Bill's partner driver claimed to have held the horse down.

The race paid off fifteen dollars money and two five dollar side bets. Bill was in seventh heaven of ecstasy. His horse was paying dividends right on the jump.

That evening the partners appeared and in a high state of excitement—at least, well feigned. They had just come from a conflab with the owner of Dusty Streak, the horse which ran second best in Shooting Star's victorious race and the "rube," just an old farmer they termed him, had declared up and down that his horse could lose Bill's in the first lap if it hadn't been that Shooting Star crowded him all over the track, with his weaving around and breaking gait every hundred paces or so. He even hinted that it was more of a running race as far as Bill's horse was concerned.

That might have sounded a little odd to a better versed race track man but Bill could hardly have qualified as a rank amateur. He took up the gauntlet in stout defense of his animal and offered to bet what was left of his hundred and fifty dollars plus the twenty-five dollars stakes of the afternoon's race.

The owner of Dusty Streak was not hard to locate and a private race was quickly arranged, Bill putting up the money while his two partners gave plenty of moral support. The race was set for the next day, and while it was entirely unofficial as far as the fair board was concerned, they gladly loaned the use

200

of the track, booking it as an extra added attraction, of which they had all too few anyway.

The news traveled around, and, as the time set approached, the small stand and track-side space were well occupied by an expectant throng. The two principals appeared and led their respective horses out onto the track and the two somewhat rickety sulkies bounced along behind over the rough ground of the trackside. Dusty Streak's owner, an insignificant, somewhat fugitive-faced little shrimp of a fellow, looked to be anything but a "rube farmer," as Bill's tall partner had scornfully referred to him.

Bill, his enthusiasm and possible optimism cooled a bit, moved about a little uneasily as the two drivers mounted their sulky seats and prepared to limber up their steeds a little before the bell. Somehow or other, Shooting Star didn't look so impressive now that nearly a hundred and fifty dollars hung in the balance. Bill's tall partner, however, reassured him that the race was practically in the bag even before it took place.

It was supposed to be another trotting heat but as Bill recalled now that phrase had scarcely been mentioned. Furthermore, although his partners had implied that Dusty Streak and his owner were strictly local and of the community, no one seemed to know either the horse or the wrinkle-faced little man who was now perched on the seat behind him.

At last the judges, who had by now entered the stand, shouted out what few particulars they had concerning the coming event and the two drivers jockeyed their outfits into position for the take-off. Twice they were forced to give the bell on trial starts because Shooting Star didn't seem to be able to make up his mind, whether he wanted to trot, pace, gallop, or just plain run, and as a result he was away behind at the starting post. The third time however he hit his stride—temporarily as it proved to be—and set off at what looked to be a compromise between a pace and a lope.

Dusty Streak either had mastered a new technique overnight or else he had just been loafing in the previous day's race, for he stretched out until he looked to be only about three feet high and almost made Shooting Star look like he was

201

standing still. It could hardly be called a race and on the second lap he was so far ahead that his driver didn't even bother to "push the lines" any further, just gave him his own head. Shooting Star was so far behind that his driver just turned him off the track and quit.

Bill stared at the debacle and turned away in a daze. His money was gone and all hopes of creating a sensation in racing circles dashed to earth. Disillusioned and dejected he waited much later at the stable for his partners to show up, but somehow he missed them, although Shooting Star was contentedly munching hay in his stall.

That night he slept on a pile of hay, and still no partners. The next day the stable attendant who had held the bet stakes, including Bill's money, intimated that he was under the impression that the two had left town, accompanied by Dusty Streak and his owner, after taking up the money. Oddly enough, the idea that there might have been collusion between Woodsley, the two recent partners, and Dusty Streak's owner didn't occur to Bill until a long time afterward.

Still more curious was the fact that he, after trading the worthless Shooting Star for four seven-and-a-half-dollar "hiders," was still obsessed with the race horse idea and approached his wife for several hundred dollars more to finance further operations. She laughed in his face, even though she hadn't heard just what happened over in Thayer County.

A few weeks later at a corn-shucking Bill was seen piloting two nondescript mules up and down the corn rows on his wife's farm. His racing career had ended about as suddenly as it started.

GLOSSARY

back-handed trade, back-trade: A trade which is reversed by reexchanging the animals, usually with one party losing whatever money or merchandise he had thrown in on the trade as **boot**

balky: *See* **cold-shouldered**

blaze(d)-face(d): Horse with large white spot on head between the eyes

blind staggers: Selenium poisoning—picked up from the soil or plants or grains grown in selenium-rich soils—causing partial blindness and staggering

boot: Whatever money, watches, whiskey, or other merchandise is added to the value of one horse to make it close enough in value to another horse to effect a trade

botts: Infestation of fly eggs, usually in open sore

bull windy: Horse with a larynx condition that causes loud, violent breathing and general debilitation

cold-shouldered: Reluctant to work or perform whatever is demanded by the driver

cribber: Horse that has the troublesome habit of chewing or biting fence wood, crib, or stall edges

cups: Grooves in the horse's teeth used to gauge age

drive single: Work one horse alone between shafts to pull a light carriage, as opposed to two or more horses on either side of a tongue for heavier loads

fistula: Abscess, **poll evil**

founders: Blood condition, caused by overfeeding and watering when the animal has been overworked, that causes permanent lameness

gant up: Be thin, emaciated, hungry, perhaps as a result of a poor or stingy owner or some physical problem of the horse itself; probably from "gaunt"

glanders: A contagious disease characterized by a swelling of the jaw glands and a runny nose

gummer: A horse so old that the teeth have worn down to the gums

Gypsy trader: Sometimes really a Gypsy but also used as a label for any roader

heaves: Also *wind-broke;* a respiratory disease characterized by very heavy breathing, snorting, coughing, and heaving flanks

heavey: With the heaves

hide-bound: So thin that the skin is pulled tight over the animal's bones

jenny: Female donkey

lampers (lampas): Swelling in mouth tissues

lump jaw: Swelling of jaw caused by sore teeth, bruised bone, any mouth infection

molder: Horse with good grinding teeth, indicating youth

moon-eyed: Moon-blind, allegedly blind during certain phases of the moon

pelter: Snide, snag, plug, worthless horse

phaeton: Light four-wheeled carriage, usually drawn by one or two horses

plug: Snide, snag, pelter, worthless horse

pole: Tongue or shaft of wagon or buggy

poll evil (polevell, poleval, polivel): Fistula or boil

rig: Wagon, buggy, or carriage

ring bone: Boney enlargement below the fetlocks

roader: Traveling professional horse trader

roarer: A horse that tends to stray or a horse with a whistling or rushing breath caused by paralysis of the larynx

scissors bits: Cruel, jointed bit that bites and pinches when the reins are handled—used primarily for difficult horses

scours: Diarrhea

shafts: Two light tongues leading forward from the buggy or wagon for a single horse between; *see also* **tongue**

shanker joints (joint ill): Possibly shigellosis, a fatal problem caused by foal not getting sufficient colostrum from dam

side bones: Hardening of the cartilage immediately above the hoof

single driver: Horse that drives well alone, between shafts

single tree: Wooden hitch bar for one or two horses on either side of a wagon tongue

skate: Snag, pelter, plug, worthless horse

skin: Snide, snag, pelter, plug, worthless horse

smooth: Attractive, good-looking

smooth-mouthed: With teeth worn down by age, ten years old or older

snag: Snide, pelter, plug, worthless horse

snide: Snag, pelter, plug, worthless horse

span: A team

spavin: Bag spavin—fluid-filled swelling on hock; bone spavin—a stiffening of the hocks much like rheumatism

splints: Bone growth and stiffening caused by overworking a horse when it is young

stifle joint: Horse's knee

stringhalt: Nerve disorder that causes swelling in hock and lameness

stump sucker: *See* **cribber**

sweenied: Overworked to the collapse of muscles under the collar or harness

switcher: Horse that switches its tail excessively, usually a result of overwork, overriding, or anxiety

tack: Harness

tongue: Single bar leading ahead from a wagon or buggy so that two horses can be hitched, one on either side of the tongue; *see also* **shafts**

tugs: Heavy leather pulling straps running back from the collar and hames

whistler: *See* **roarer**

wind-broke: *See* **heaves**

wind choker: *See* **heaves**

wind sucker: *See* **heaves**

youth spots: Light-colored spots that fade as horse matures

BIBLIOGRAPHY

Bailey, James M. *Life in Danbury.* Boston: Shepard and Gill, 1873.

Barnum, R. C. *The People's Home Library.* Cleveland: R. C. Barnum Co., 1914.

Conrad, Earl. *Horse Trader.* New York: Thomas Y. Crowell, 1953.

Ferris, William R., Jr. "Ray Lum: Muletrader." *North Carolina Folklore* 21, (1973): 105–19.

Jansen, William Hugh. "Down Our Way: Who'll Bid Twenty?" *Kentucky Folklore Record* 2, (1956): 113–21.

Lomax, Alan. *The Folk Songs of North America* Garden City, N.Y.: Doubleday, 1960.

Marryatt, Capt. Frederick. *Diary in America.* Bloomington: Indiana University Press, 1960.

Queen, Myra. "Horse Trading." *In Foxfire 4,* edited by Eliot Wigginton, pp. 215–21. Garden City, N.Y.: Doubleday, Anchor Books, 1977.

Randolph, Vance. *Ozark Folksongs.* Columbia: State Historical Society of Missouri, 1949.

Sylvester, B. F. "Hoss Tradin'." The *Saturday Evening Post,* 6 January 1934, p. 12.

Welsch, Roger L. *Shingling the Fog and Other Plains Lies.* Chicago: Swallow Press, 1972.

Welsch, Roger L. *A Treasury of Nebraska Pioneer Folklore.* Lincoln: University of Nebraska Press, 1966.